# Values Are Forever

## Becoming More Caring and Responsible

**Gary A. Davis**



**Westwood Publishing Company**
**Cross Plains, Wisconsin 53528**

**About the Author.** Gary A. Davis is Professor Emeritus of the University of Wisconsin, Department of Educational Psychology, in Madison, Wisconsin. He is author of several college textbooks, including *Creativity is Forever* (Kendall/Hunt), *Education of the Gifted and Talented* (with Sylvia Rimm; Allyn & Bacon), and *Handbook of Gifted Education* (with Nicholas Colangelo; Allyn & Bacon). In the values area, *Teaching Values* (also a Westwood book) is a 300-page idea book for teachers (or parents) of students in grades 4–8, or younger or older. The author's interest in children's values was born largely in listening to daily teenage tragedies on station WBBM Chicago. Many of these disasters might have been prevented by helping children—at a younger age—logically understand values that are helpful versus hurtful, productive versus self-destructive.

ISBN 1-888115-00-9

Library of Congress Catalog Card Number: 95-90784

How to Order:
Single or multiple copies may be ordered from Westwood Publishing Company, P. O. Box 222, Cross Plains, WI 53528. Telephone (608) 798-1040. Quantity discounts available. On letterhead stationary, indicate intended use of the books (personal or classroom copy, resale, library) and include purchase order number, check, money order, or credit card type (VISA/MC) and number and expiration date.

Dear Teacher or Parent,

The mission of *Values Are Forever: Becoming More Caring and Responsible* is to help children and youth ages 9 to 12—or younger or older—understand what values are and discover why positive, constructive values are essential to their present, teenage, and adult lives. The activities and exercises help children:

- ✔ Think logically about values and behavior.
- ✔ Empathize with others.
- ✔ Discover for themselves why some values are helpful and others are hurtful—to others and themselves.
- ✔ Value self-respect and respect from others.
- ✔ Make personal commitments to constructive values.
- ✔ Shape their identities of who they are and what kind of human beings they wish to become.

*Values Are Forever* also helps children grasp how poor values can make life difficult, and in some cases can trash their lives. The workbook helps children think logically about *honesty, fair play, empathy, compassion, rights of others, responsibility, actions and consequences, education, good health, pleasantness, self-respect, and respect from others.*

Many of the values and exercises relate to teenage problems. It is essential that children be prepared in advance for the values questions that teenagers face. When they become teenagers, it may be too late.

The solution to America's values crisis is not building more prisons. The solution is helping children—tomorrow's teenagers and adults—understand and embrace values that are advantageous to themselves and to others. Today's children are tomorrow's responsible and productive adults. Some of today's children are tomorrow's dangerous and destructive teenagers and adults.

*Values Are Forever* seeks to help children and youth create better futures for themselves, and become better citizens for all of society.

Dear Young Person:

This book is about YOU and YOUR LIFE.

It will help you think about these kinds of questions:

> What kind of person do you want to be?
> Do you want people to RESPECT you?
> Do you want people to LIKE you?
> How do you want to live your life?
> Do you want to be successful?
> Do you want to feel good about YOURSELF?

You are a VERY IMPORTANT person.

> You are important to your family.
> You are important to your teachers.
> You are important to your neighborhood.
> Especially, you are important to YOU.

Think.
Use that computer between your ears.
Be the best person you can be.
Live your life in a way that's best for you.
And best for others.

You have ONE life to live.
ONE chance to do it right.
Don't mess it up.

# Contents

Chapter

# 1

# Decisions and Choices:

## Should I Eat Cheerios or Become a Criminal?



We make decisions every day.

Some Decisions are little decisions.

"Little decisions" will not affect your life. At least not very much.

These are some little decisions:

- Should I eat Cheerios or Mini-Wheats for breakfast?
- Which shirt will I wear to school today?
- Should I tie my shoes or let them flop open?
- Should I take my yellow pencil or my green one?

- For lunch should I have a hot dog or a slice of pizza?
- Should I rest on my left elbow or my right elbow?
- Should I buy the red gym shorts or the blue ones?
- Should I eat some Peanut M & Ms or plain M & Ms?

Mom and the neighbors make little decisions too:

- Should I buy the blouse with the long sleeves or the short sleeves?
- Should we have spaghetti for dinner or chicken soup?
- Should I go shopping Saturday morning or Saturday afternoon?

Little Decisions will NOT affect:

WHO YOU ARE.

HOW YOU SEE YOURSELF.

WHAT PEOPLE THINK OF YOU (at least not much).

YOUR CHANCES FOR A GOOD FUTURE LIFE.

WHAT YOU WILL BECOME.

Some Decisions are **BIG DECISIONS.**

They are "BIG DECISIONS" because they affect your WHOLE LIFE. They affect WHO YOU ARE. Some BIG DECISIONS can trash your life. Permanently.

These are some BIG DECISIONS:

- Should I be DISHONEST? Should I steal things from people's desks, lockers, or coat pockets?
- Should I steal things from the department store, the drug store, and the record store?
- Should I tell lots of lies and break promises?
- Should I borrow things and never return them?
- Or should I be an HONEST person? Should I be someone that people trust and respect?

- Should I be someone that I can respect?

- Should I be rude and loud? Should I yell at people? Shoot off my mouth in class? Put people down every chance I get? ("Don't be so dumb, Jason!" "What an ugly shirt, Lashanda!")
- Should I have a bad temper and be grouchy? Should I snap at my parents, my friends, and my teacher when I feel like it?
- Or should I be pleasant and help people? Should I give compliments? ("Good idea, Jason!" "Nice shirt, Lashanda!")

- Should I be lazy in school? Should I try to avoid work? Should I try NOT to learn anything?
- Should I plan to drop out of school as soon as I can?
- Or should I try hard to learn in school? Should I learn important skills? Should I learn about my world? (With an education, it's easier to get a good job after high school. It's even better to go on to a technical school or college.)

- Should I be a bully? Should I push little kids around? Should I make them give me their money?
- Or should I think about what it's like to be bullied? Then I would not be a bully.

- Should I ignore my health? Should I eat lots of junk? Not get any exercise (except pushing TV buttons)? Start smoking right away?
- Or should I take care of my body, eat well, and get lots of exercise? Go to the dentist every day? Maybe get on the soccer and soft ball teams. And live healthier and probably longer. (Just kidding about the dentist. Twice a year is best.)

- Should I plan to become a criminal when I am 16 or 17? Maybe 12 or 13? Should I learn how to rob Stop-And-Go Stores? How to be a burglar? Should I plan to spend my life in prison?
- Or should I learn values that will help me live a better life?

**BIG DECISIONS are the important ones.**

BIG DECISIONS AFFECT:

**Who We Are:** We can enjoy who we are. We can respect ourselves. Or we can end up just wishing we would have made better decisions.

**How We See Ourselves:** We can be proud of ourselves. We can be proud of what we do with our lives.
Or we can end up wishing we would have been more careful.

**How Others See Us:** We can decide to be pleasant, honest, and willing to work for what we want. If we do that, others will respect us. If we make bad decisions—and become unpleasant, dishonest, and uneducated—we lose respect.

**What We Will Become:** If we make good decisions, our lives probably will be more successful, more enjoyable, and EASIER.

**A lot of middle school and high school students make BIG DECISIONS that hurt themselves.**

For example:

- Some are unpleasant, grouchy, nasty, messy people whom nobody likes. Except other unpleasant, grouchy, nasty, messy people.
- Many of them drop out of school—and then are unhappy because they need money, but can't get a good job.
- A few bring a gun to school because they think it's cool and it makes them feel "tough" and "powerful."
- Some ruin their health. They take drugs, drink a lot of booze, smoke a pack a day, and maybe catch some bad diseases.
- Some become criminals and go to prison.
- Some sell drugs, because they think they will get lots of money. They end up in prison too. If they don't get shot dead by the "tough" kids who carry guns.
- Some teenagers join gangs. Gang members tell each other that it's cool to have a gun. It's cool to drop out of school. It's cool to sell drugs and become a criminal. It's cool to scare everybody in the neighborhood. Sometimes they shoot members of other gangs.

> **More than half of all gang members end up in prison—or dead—before they are 25 years old!**

Some teenagers don't even THINK about job skills. Or professional training. After high school, they have BIG trouble finding a good job or career.

Other middle-school and high-school students make better BIG DECISIONS.

- They want to like themselves.
- They want others to respect them.
- They want to make a good life for themselves and their future families.

Do you see the difference?

Little decisions don't make much difference. ("Should I buy chocolate or strawberry ice cream—who cares?")

BIG DECISIONS can mess up your life! ("I'm going to drop out of school. I'm going to make big bucks selling marijuana and crack cocaine!")

Chapter

# 2

# Little Decisions, Big Decisions:

## Which Are Which?

Let's make sure you understand little decisions and BIG DECISIONS.

If the statement is a little decision (which doesn't make much difference), put a "✓" under "little decision." If the statement is a BIG DECISION (that affects *who you are, what others think of you*, and *what might happen to you*), put a "✓" under "BIG DECISION."

| | Little Decision | **Big** Decision |
|---|---|---|
| 1. Shalena decides that it is all right to steal things from other children. | ☐ | ☐ |
| 2. Justin decides that since it's Tuesday, he should walk to school on the left side of the street instead of the right side. | ☐ | ☐ |
| 3. Carlos criticizes, complains, and grouches at everybody. Carlos has decided to be a mean and nasty person with a bad temper—ALWAYS. | ☐ | ☐ |
| 4. Marie has decided that school is too much work. She says "School is for suckers and dopes. I'm going to drop out when I am a teenager!" | ☐ | ☐ |
| 5. Darnell has decided to join a gang just as soon as he can. He thinks gangs are cool. He thinks gang jackets are wonderful. He thinks gang members will be such good friends. And he can carry a gun. "And if I get mad at somebody, maybe I'll just blow 'em away!" | ☐ | ☐ |
| 6. Chelsea is worried about her hair. "Should I leave it long? Or should I cut it a little shorter?" | ☐ | ☐ |
| 7. Jeremy does not care about being an honest person. Jeremy decided to lie, cheat, and steal whenever he wants. | ☐ | ☐ |

| | Little Decision | **Big** Decision |
|---|---|---|
| 8. Tanya decided that it's all right to break promises and leaves messes in class and at home. She decided that it's all right if nobody trusts her. | ☐ | ☐ |
| 9. Robert got some money for his birthday. "Should I buy a radio-controlled pickup truck from Radio Shack? Or a sweat shirt that says Green Bay Packers on it?" | ☐ | ☐ |
| 10. After days of worrying, Consuela decided, "I really like strawberry ice cream better than chocolate!" | ☐ | ☐ |

**Score**: You can score yourself. Some decisions little ones that don't make much difference in your life (2, 6, 9, 10). Other decisions are BIG ones. BIG DECISIONS affect who you are. How you see yourself. What you will become. What people think of you. BIG DECISIONS affect your chances for a good future life (1, 3, 4, 5, 7, 8).

Did you get a perfect score?

# Values:

## What's Good and Bad About Them?

---

The BIG decisions we talked about are related to *your values.*

### OUR VALUES . . .

- ➔ Are our own ideas about what is RIGHT and what is WRONG.
- ➔ Are part of WHO we are.
- ➔ Are OUR OWN RULES that we live by.
- ➔ Guide our DECISIONS and what we DO.
- ➔ Affect our FEELINGS about others and ourselves.
- ➔ Determine how GOOD our LIVES will become.
- ➔ Guide us in making little decisions and BIG decisions.

Values guide what we think and do.

- If we value HONESTY, we do not steal.
- If we value HELPFULNESS, we will help people.

- If we value FRIENDLINESS, we will try to pleasant and likable.
- If we value our HEALTH, we will be careful about what we eat and drink, we will exercise, and we will try to avoid diseases.
- If we value WHAT OTHERS THINK OF US, we will try to be trustworthy.
- If we value FAIRNESS, we will treat others the way we would like them to treat us.
- If we value BEING CONSIDERATE with others, we will be polite, return things, and not leave messes for mom, the teacher, or the school custodian to clean up.
- If we value WHO WE ARE and HOW WE WILL LIVE OUR FUTURE LIVES, we will try to become educated and trained.

We can tell a LOT about YOUR values by what you do.

| **If you:** | **We know that you:** |
|---|---|
| Break promises, lie, cheat, and steal | Do not value being honest, fair, and trustworthy. |
| Toss papers and junk on hall floors and dump garbage on the lunch room floor | Do not value a clean, attractive environment.<br>Do not care about making more work for the custodian. |
| Break school windows and spray paint the bus stop | Do not respect public property.<br>Do not value beauty.<br>Do not wish to be trustworthy.<br>Do not think about others' rights. |

| If you: | We know that you: |
| --- | --- |
| Are friendly, help people, and maybe even send birthday cards | Value friendliness, helpfulness, and thoughtfulness. |

Chapter

# 4

# Word Search About Values:

## (Now Where the Heck Is *GOOD?*)

---

Have you done word search puzzles?

In this puzzle, words related to values are hidden in the block of letters.

The words can be printed left to right or top to bottom. One word is printed backwards—right to left.

Find the following words and draw a ring around them

| | | |
|---|---|---|
| Education | Honest | Fair |
| Right | Friendly | Thoughtful |
| Good | Trustworthy | Health |
| Values | Helpful | Wrong |

| A | F | K | F | T | U | Z | J | Y | P | O |
|---|---|---|---|---|---|---|---|---|---|---|
| T | R | U | S | T | W | O | R | T | H | Y |
| W | I | X | G | H | B | V | I | H | E | E |
| H | E | D | O | O | G | A | G | N | L | D |
| O | N | C | G | U | D | L | H | C | P | U |
| N | D | L | Q | G | F | U | T | Z | F | C |
| E | L | Q | I | H | Y | E | X | M | U | A |
| S | Y | G | J | T | R | S | W | S | L | T |
| T | R | W | H | F | A | I | R | V | K | I |
| X | Z | Y | E | U | W | R | O | N | G | O |
| I | H | E | A | L | T | H | D | M | B | N |

The solution is at the end of the book.

Chapter

# 5

# Values:

## What Makes Good Ones Good? What Makes Bad Ones No-Goodniks?

---

The best way to make decisions about values—about what is right and what is wrong—is to ask yourself these questions:

- → Does this hurt other people?
- → Does it hurt me?
- → Can it hurt my life?
- → If I do this, will my family, my friends, and other people lose respect for me?

If the answer to ANY of these questions is "Yes," whatever it is, it's probably NOT a good idea.

It's probably a bad decision, based on no-goodnik values.

Or you can turn the questions around:

- ➔ Will this help other people or make them happier?
- ➔ Will it make my life better or happier?
- ➔ Will my family, friends, and others respect me if I do this?
- ➔ Would it be OK with mother, grandmother, my teacher, or the President of the U.S. if I do this?

If the answer to any of these questions is "No," it's probably NOT a good idea.

Chapter

# 6

# Actions and Consequences:

## "Gee Whiz, Maybe I Shouldn't Have Done That!"

---

We can look at values another way.

What we do is called our ACTIONS.
What happens from our actions is called CONSEQUENCES.

| ACTIONS → CONSEQUENCES |
|---|

**Actions have consequences.**

Consequences can be GOOD (for others or yourself).
Consequences can be BAD (for others or yourself).

Some young people—thousands, in fact—commit robberies and murders *without thinking of the consequences.*

> They hurt OTHER PEOPLE.
> They hurt OTHER PEOPLE's FAMILIES.
> They hurt THEMSELVES—probably PERMANENTLY—because they spend their lives in prison. (Prison is not a nice place to live.)

They hurt THEIR OWN FAMILIES. Their families are sad because the young person hurt someone else. Their families are sad because the young person also hurt himself or herself.

> **Different people have different values.**
> **Different values lead to different actions.**
> **Different actions have different consequences.**

☺ Some people value a good EDUCATION and good CAREER TRAINING. They "go for it!"

☹ Other people do not. Maybe they value "doing things their own way." Maybe they value "not being told what to do." Maybe they just don't THINK about what they want out of life.

☺ Some people will return a purse when they find it. They value HONESTY. They take pride in being honest.

☹ Other people will keep the money and credit cards. They value a few dollars more than being an honest person.

☺ Some people value FAIR PLAY and DEMOCRACY. They are nice to everyone, regardless of race or religion. They share with everyone. They give everyone a chance to play in games. They play fair.

☹ Other people don't value fairness. They are not nice to students who are different. They do not play fair in games.

- ☺ Some people value RESPECT from others. They also value SELF-RESPECT. They try to be pleasant, polite, and helpful. They think of themselves as helpful and likable.
- ☹ Other people don't value respect from others. They don't value self-respect, either. They treat others rudely. They blast their boom boxes in public. They throw burger wrappers out of the car window. They are rude, noisy, messy, and a pain in the neck. (Most people don't like to be around them, except other rude, noisy, messy, pain-in-the-neck people.)

Chapter

# 7

# A Quiz About Your Values

Let's see if you can tell which are "helpful" values and which are "hurtful" values.

Let's take the following quiz.

For each question:

Check "Good Value" if the action

- ➔ HELPS other people.
- ➔ HELPS yourself.
- ➔ HELPS you respect yourself.
- ➔ HELPS others to respect you. Causes them to think you are a "good person."

Check "Bad Value" if the action

- ➔ HURTS other people.
- ➔ HURTS you, your self-respect, your future, or your health.
- ➔ Causes others to lose respect for you. Causes them to think you are NOT a very pleasant or trustworthy person.

| | Good ☺Value | Bad ☹Value |
|---|---|---|
| 1. You will be a teen-ager soon, and it's time to act "grown up"—and start smoking. | ☐ | ☐ |
| 2. You decide it's best to be fair. You take turns in games. You share things. You let everyone help decide what to do. | ☐ | ☐ |
| 3. When you use the school rest-rooms, you draw and scribble on the walls. You toss waste paper on the floor. You know the custodian will have to clean up your mess. | ☐ | ☐ |
| 4. Imagine you live in North Dakota. It just snowed 8 inches. Your 80-year old neighbor is starting to shovel her sidewalk. You shovel it for her, because you believe in helpfulness. | ☐ | ☐ |
| 5. You shovel it for her because you also respect elderly people (and you can imagine what it is like to be older and weaker). | ☐ | ☐ |

| | Good ☺ Value | Bad ☹ Value |
|---|---|---|
| 6. You shovel it for her because you know you will feel REAL good about helping someone in need. You will be proud of yourself. | ☐ | ☐ |
| 7. You don't care about your elderly neighbor and her problems. You don't care what she thinks of you. So you tell her you will shovel her walk if she will pay you $5. | ☐ | ☐ |
| 8. You ignore your neighbor and her snow, because you need to think about yourself—you need to watch TV or phone somebody. (Her snow isn't your problem!) | ☐ | ☐ |

| | Good ☺ Value | Bad ☹ Value |
|---|---|---|
| 9. When you go into drugstores, you mess up the magazine rack. When you go into department stores, you mess up the neat stacks of clothes. The clerks have to clean up your messes, but you don't care. | ☐ | ☐ |
| 10. Imagine you are 16 and riding in a car with friends. You just finished your Big Mac, with a soda. You pitch your wrappers and drink cup out the car window. | ☐ | ☐ |
| 11. You are at your friend Pat's house. You see a cassette tape of your favorite rock group. When Pat isn't looking, you stick it in your your pocket. You say "Well, gotta go now." | ☐ | ☐ |
| 12. Actually, you value friends and you value being trustworthy. You help Pat with some math problems. You don't steal anything. Then you buy Pat an ice cream cone at McDonald's. | ☐ | ☐ |
| 13. When you are at McDonald's, you and Pat yell at each other across the restaurant. You use really bad swear words, so that the elderly people will know that you don't care about their rights. | ☐ | ☐ |

| | Good ☺ Value | Bad ☹ Value |
|---|---|---|
| 14. Actually, you respect the elderly. You smile and say "Hello" to them. You hold the door open for them. They smile and say "Thank you." They think you are a nice person. | ☐ | ☐ |
| 15. You think way, way ahead about your life. You do not want to spend your life in jail. You do not want to be poor. You want to have a good job or career. You know you must complete high school. Then you want to go to a technical college or a university. | ☐ | ☐ |

| | Good ☺Value | Bad ☹Value |
|---|---|---|
| 16. You think way, way ahead about WHO and WHAT you want to be when you grow up—a successful and happy person who is able to enjoy life. | ☐ | ☐ |

There ARE right and wrong answers to these values questions.

How are your values?
Are you looking out for the feelings of others?
Do you want to be fair to others?
Do you value self-respect and respect from others?
Are you thinking about "What kind of human being am I?"
Are you thinking about "What kind of human being do I wish to become?"

Chapter

# 8

# Values Sometimes Conflict:

## Is It Homework? Or Hangin' Out with Friends?

---

Sometimes values "conflict" with each other.
When values conflict, one value will tell you to do one thing. But another value tells you to do something else.

Lots of problems are caused when values conflict with each other. It happens a lot. Maybe every day.

Here are some examples:

1. You value *friends* and like to talk to them. You also value *promptness*. But talking to friends can make you late to your classroom.

2. Imagine you are a teenager who values *"being cool."* Your friends offer you a cigarette. They say, "Have a drag, smoking is cool!" But you know darn well that smoking is REAL bad for your health. And you value your *health*!

3. You value *entertainment*, and want to go to a movie. But you also value *helping mom*. You value doing what mom says. And mom wants you to clean up that big pile of garbage (you know, the one in your room!).
4. You value *doing well in school*, which means doing homework. But you also value *playing with friends, playing computer games*, and *watching TV*.
5. You value *playing music*. But you also value *being a good neighbor*, which means not disturbing others with music that is too loud.
6. When you become a teenager, you probably will value being a *member of a group*. And some friends might want you to join their gang—and take drugs and steal things. But you also value *honesty* and—especially—having a *good future life*.

Some value conflicts are fairly easy to solve.

☞ You can *choose one or the other.*

"Sorry, I can't play right now. I really need to do my math homework."

"No thanks, no cigarettes. I might need my lungs for breathing."

"Sorry, no gangs, no drugs, no stealing. I want a better life than that!"

☞ You can *work out a compromise.* ("Compromise" means "something in-between.")

"I can't talk to you now because I'll be late. Meet me at lunch time, we'll talk then."

"Mom, I'll clean my room in a hurry—if I can go to the movie, OK?"

"I'll use headphones so my music won't disturb anyone."

"Instead of a gang, I'll find a better group to join. Maybe a softball, soccer, or basketball team, or a church or synagogue group."

☞ You can find a *completely new solution.*

"I don't need to smoke to be 'cool.' I'll be cool and well-liked by being a helpful, friendly person."

"I'll do homework first thing—then reward myself with an hour of computer games!"

**Sometimes it helps to ask yourself:**
**"Which choice is best (more important) for other people?"**
**"Which choice is best (more important) for myself?"**

Being prompt is more important that a few more words with friends (you'll see them later anyway).
Your health is more important than smelly, expensive cigarettes.
Helping mom is more important than watching TV.
Homework comes first, watching TV is second.

It also helps to talk to someone. Maybe mom, dad, a brother or sister, another relative, a teacher, or a neighbor can help you make the best choice.

Let's practice thinking about some values conflicts:

**1. Soccer or a Party?**

Imagine you are on the soccer team. A BIG championship game is coming up. The coach wants a team practice at 2:00 p.m. on Saturday. But you also are invited to a GREAT birthday party at exactly the same time! You value sports AND parties.

What are the advantages of going to the soccer practice?

______________________________________________

______________________________________________

What are the advantages of going to the party?

______________________________________________

______________________________________________

Which is most important? (Or are they equally important?)

______________________________________________

Now the hard part: What would you do?

*Will you choose one?*
Maybe you feel that the soccer practice is really the most important.

*Can you find a compromise?*
Maybe you could ask the coach if you could leave practice early. Then you could go to the party a little late.

*Can you find a new solution?*
Maybe you could ask the coach to work with you from 1:00 to 2:30. Then go to the party.

*Can you talk to someone* about this decision?
The coach? Other players?

How might you solve this conflict?

________________________________________

________________________________________

## 2. Friendship or Honesty?

Your best friend Christopher steals a valuable microscope from school. He tells you about it. You value your friendship with Christopher. But you also value honesty. You know that teachers and other students need that microscope. You have to decide: Should you tell a teacher or not?

What are the advantages of not telling anyone?

________________________________________

________________________________________

What are the advantages of telling a teacher about Christopher?

________________________________________

________________________________________

The hard part: What would you do?

*Can you choose one solution?*
Would you keep quiet, because Christopher is your friend?
Or would you tell a teacher—"spill the beans"—because you know Christopher is wrong? You know that the school needs that microscope.

*Can you find a compromise?*
Maybe you could ask Christopher to use the microscope for just a few days, then return it.

*Can you find a new solution?*
Maybe you could offer to help Christopher pay for a new microscope, if he will return the one he stole?

*Can you talk to someone* about making this values conflict?
Mom? A big brother or sister? Another friend?

What would you do?

______________________________________________

### 3. Family or Yourself?

You value your family. You also value going for bike rides, going to the mall, and playing games and sports with friends. Your mom and dad want to take you to visit Aunt Jennifer EVERY Saturday. Aunt Jennifer lives alone and is not well.

How do you feel about this?

______________________________________

______________________________________

______________________________________

Can you think of a *compromise*? Can you think of other ways to show Aunt Jennifer you care about her?

______________________________________________

______________________________________________

______________________________________________

Remember: For ALL values conflicts, think about:

What is truly best for OTHER PEOPLE.
What is truly best for YOURSELF.
What is the RIGHT thing to do.

Make careful choices.
Compromise.
Look for new ideas.
Talk to people about the problem.

**Ask yourself: What would someone with good values do? ☺**

Chapter

# Big Value Conflicts:

## Let's Talk Money!

Let's talk about MONEY.
Let's talk about education, a future job, and your future life.

Maybe you have heard people say,

"Oh, money isn't the most important thing in life."

Or maybe,

"Money can't buy happiness."

Both of these statements are TRUE. Some rich people are not happy.

But think about this:
When you grow up, AT THE VERY LEAST:

- ☞ You will need a place to live.
- ☞ You will need food on the table.
- ☞ You will want to do fun things once in a while.
- ☞ And you probably will need a car.

$50 $50

All of these take MONEY—cash, currency, bills, moolah, green stuff, cabbage, legal tender, coin-of-the-realm.

$50 $50

Monopoly Money doesn't do it.
Robbery and selling drugs doesn't do it (unless your idea of "a place to live" and "food on the table" is the State Prison).

Most adults want more than "THE VERY LEAST."
Most want a comfortable, nice place to live.
Most want to eat healthy meals. And go out to dinner once in a while.
Most want to buy nice clothes.
Most want a vacation once in a while. ("Disneyland, here we come!")
Most want a nice car, or maybe two (for the family).

**Money can help you have comforts, opportunities, and choices.**

**To live well, everyone must know how to make money.**

THE SURE WAY TO MAKE MONEY IS EDUCATION AND TRAINING.
It feels good to learn a skill or trade.

It feels good to be really good at something. Like being a carpenter, welder, secretary, nurse, truck driver, electrician, store manager, teacher, doctor, or business executive.

So let's talk education and training.
And YOU can figure it out for yourself!

Put a smile face by the best answer. ☺

1. Which is the BEST way to get a job that you like? A job that pays good money?

   - ☐ Don't study; drop out of high school.
   - ☐ Graduate from high school; then go to a technical school or a college.

2. Pat and Chris are in high school. In the following sketches, who is REALLY cool, Pat or Chris? Who "thinks ahead"? Who probably will make a better life for himself or herself?

   - ☐ Pat loves athletics. Pat NEVER studies. Pat just practices soccer, basketball, and softball. Pat NEVER thinks beyond high school. Pat NEVER thinks about a career and earning money.

☐ Chris loves athletics too. Chris practices basketball, tennis, and running—but Chris does homework and gets good grades (so Chris can get into college or a technical school).

3. Your parents will say "Stay in school." "Get an education." "Don't drive drunk." "Don't smoke!" And "Drugs will hurt your body and get you into trouble!"

☐ Your parents are older and smarter. They've "been there." You should listen to them!

☐ When you get to be 13, 14, or 15, you will be a lot smarter than your parents. You might plan to drop out of school, stay drunk, smoke a lot, and take drugs if you feel like it.

4. You are a 16-year old girl. You dropped out of high school and had *three babies before you were 21*. Your husband was unhappy and left you. You have no job skills. The money that the state gives you is not enough for rent and food. You cannot afford a car or new clothes.

- [ ] You have a wonderful life and would not change a thing.
- [ ] You probably wish you had done things differently when you were in high school.

Check all of the following that are your goals when you are an adult:

- [ ] Nice house
- [ ] Nice car
- [ ] Nice clothes
- [ ] Happy family life
- [ ] Enough extra money to pay for entertainment, vacations, keeping your teeth fixed, and other things.

Think about what is truly best for other people and best for YOURSELF—for the rest of your life.

**Make careful choices.**
**You only have one life to live.**
**Make it GOOD!**
**DON'T mess it up.**

**GO FOR IT!**

Chapter

# 10

# Barnstorming . . . I Mean Brainwashing . . . I Mean Brainstorming:

## About Friendliness

Have you done brainstorming in your classes? Brainstorming helps you think of creative ideas.

The most important brainstorming rule is:

**Think of all the ideas you can.**

Here is the situation:

Imagine that Maria Gonzales is a new student in your classroom. Maria is from Colombia, in South America.

How many ways can you think of to show FRIENDLINESS to Maria? What can you do to show Maria that you are glad she is in your class? How can you show Maria that you like her?

If you were Maria, in a new school, how would you like to be treated?

Check one:

☐ Rudely and unpleasantly.

☐ In friendly and respectful ways.

Chapter

# 11

# Reverse Brainstorming:

## How Can We Make Things Worse?

---

Have you heard of REVERSE BRAINSTORMING?
It's a little strange.

**With Reverse Brainstorming, you think of ideas to make something WORSE!**

Reverse Brainstorming helps us to understand a problem better.

Here's the problem: How many ways can you DESTROY your health? Use your imagination. Think about how teenagers or grown-ups ruin their health.

______________________________________________

______________________________________________

______________________________________________

______________________________________________

______________________________________________

______________________________________________

________________________________________

________________________________________

________________________________________

________________________________________

Which will help you live a better life?

Check one: ☐ Good health

☐ Sickness, weakness, and bad health

Chapter

# 12

# More Reverse Brainstorming:

## Imagine That You Are a Lying, Cheating, Stealing, Dishonest CREEP!

Let's do another reverse brainstorming problem.

How can you show that you NOT a trustworthy person? How can you prove to people that you are a lying, cheating, stealing, dishonest creep? Think of all the ideas you can.

Do you want people to trust you? Yes ☐ No ☐

Do you want people to respect you? Yes ☐ No ☐

Should you REALLY do the things on your list? Yes ☐ No ☐

Chapter

# 13

# Arithmetic Test:

## "Let's Subtract Tyler!"

---

Imagine that Tyler is a dishonest, unfair person. You might call him a *crook*. Tyler steals everything. He lies to everybody. He cheats in every game. He breaks promises. He vandalizes and breaks other people's things. And he NEVER returns anything!

Here are some arithmetic problems about Tyler.
The answers are at the end of this chapter.

1. You have 4 friends, Jackie, Latricia, Bobbie—and Tyler.

   a. How many *good* friends to you have? ______
   b. How many friends can you trust? ______

Jackie, Latricia, Bobbie, Tyler

— Tyler

---

?

2. You received 8 new cassettes for your birthday. Tyler comes over for a visit. Now you have 6 new cassettes. How many cassettes do you believe are in Tyler's pocket? _____

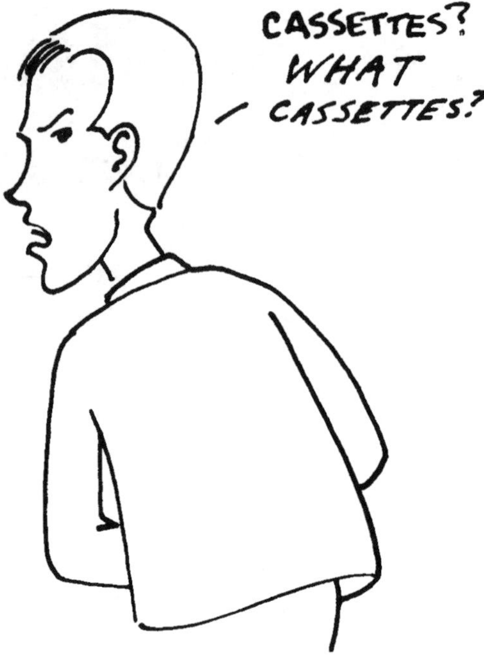


3. Your teacher, Mr. Gonzales, gives you a spelling test. There are 10 words. Then he asks five people (you, Jackie, Latricia, Bobbie, and Tyler) how many words you spelled correctly. (It was a hard test.)

   You say "7."
   Jackie says "8."
   Latricia says "6."
   Bobbie says "7."
   Tyler says "10—I got 'em ALL right!"

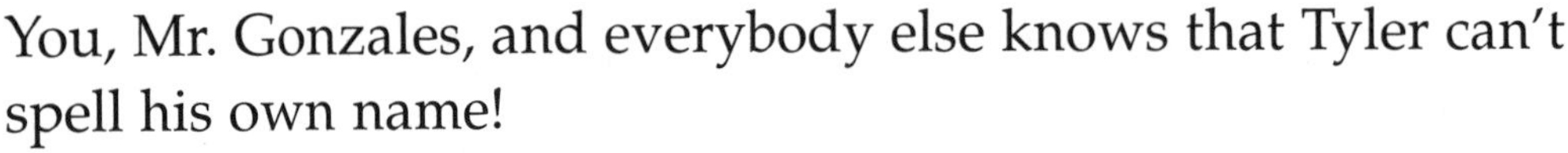

   You, Mr. Gonzales, and everybody else knows that Tyler can't spell his own name!

   a. How many people will think Tyler is a dishonest liar? (Don't forget yourself and Mr. Gonzales.) ______
   b. How many people will lose respect for Tyler? ______

Here's how Tyler usually spells:

**"Misster rabit ayt hiz carotz."**

4. On Monday Jackie loans five valuable books. Jackie loans one to you, one to Latricia—and three to Tyler. Jackie asks all of you to return them on Thursday. On Friday, how many books does Jackie have? ______

5. You are getting smarter about friends. Of Jackie, Latricia, Bobbie, and Tyler, how many are no longer your friends?

   ______

6. Imagine that you, Jackie, Latricia, Bobbie, and Tyler are in high school. Tyler drops out and watches TV all day. The rest of you graduate, and go on to college or a technical school.

   a. When you are all 30 years old, how many will have a good job and earn good pay? (Don't forget to count yourself.)

      ______

   b. How many will WISH they had stayed in school? ______

7. Tyler has some new friends. Two of them are burglars and steal things. Two others sell drugs. Two more break windows, set fires, and chop down little trees at the school.

a. How many will probably be arrested by the police? (Don't include Tyler, yet.) ______
b. How many will be embarrassed and feel awful when the police talk to their parents? ______
c. How many might be sent to a juvenile detention center? ______

Do you RESPECT Tyler?
Yes _____ No _____

Would you like to BE like Tyler?
Yes _____ No _____

Would the world be a mess if EVERYONE were like Tyler?
Yes _____ No _____

Answers to arithmetic problems:

1a. 3 1b. 3 2. 2 3a. 5 3b. 5

4. 2 5. 1 6a. 4 6b. 1 7a. 6

7b. 6 7c. 6

Chapter

# 14

# "What Would Happen If ...

## Everyone Were Dishonest?"

---

Do you sometimes imagine "What would happen if . . . ?"

Like "What would happen if it were winter all the time?"
Or "What would happen if I broke my leg?"
Or "What would happen if we moved to Hollywood?"
Or "What would happen if we were invaded by giant worms from outer space?"

We can Brainstorm ideas for problems that begin with "What would happen if . . . ?"

Do you remember "Actions" and "Consequences"?
What we DO is our *actions*.
What happens as a RESULT of what we do is *consequences*.
Consequences can be *good* for others and ourselves.
Or consequences can be *bad* for others and ourselves.

> **"What would happen if . . . ?" problems help us to think about CONSEQUENCES of ACTIONS. If we think about CONSEQUENCES, maybe we will be careful about our ACTIONS.**

Let's try this "What would happen if . . . ?" problem:

In the last chapter we talked about Tyler. Tyler is BAD NEWS. He is dishonest and unfair. He steals everything that isn't nailed down. He lies. He cheats. He breaks promises. He vandalizes. He does not return anything he borrows!

(And he probably does not say "Please" and "Thank you.")

What would happen if EVERYONE in your school were like Tyler. That is, EVERYONE is a dishonest and unfair person. Everyone lies, steals, cheats, and breaks promises. Everyone makes messes and trashes the school. Everyone cheats on tests, doesn't do homework, and never returns anything.

What would school be like?
What would friendships be like?
What would stores be like?
What would families be like?

What would happen if everyone were like Tyler?

_______________________________________________________________________

_______________________________________________________________________

_______________________________________________________________________

_______________________________________________________________________

_______________________________________________________________________

_______________________________________________________________________

_______________________________________________________________________

_______________________________________________________________________

_______________________________________________________________________

_______________________________________________________________________

Are you glad everyone is NOT like Tyler?

Yes _____ No _____

Are you glad YOU are not like Tyler?

Yes _____ No _____

Chapter

# 15

# Understanding Feelings (Empathy):

## Is It Fun To Get Hurt?

---

It is IMPORTANT to understand how other people feel.

- ➔ If you understand how someone feels when they are sad, you probably won't try to make them sad.
- ➔ If you understand how someone feels when their feelings are hurt, you probably won't try to hurt their feelings?
- ➔ If you understand how someone feels when something is stolen from them, you probably will not steal their things.
- ➔ If you understand how someone feels when they are cheated, you probably will not cheat them.
- ➔ If you understand how it feels to have your nose hurt, you probably won't sock somebody in the nose.

WHY? Because:

YOU do not like to feel sad.
YOU do not like to have your feelings hurt.
YOU do not like to have your things stolen.
YOU do not like to be cheated.
YOU do not like to be socked in the nose.

Here is a terrific word for you: **Empathy**

If we "have empathy," that means we understand someone's feelings.
We know how they feel.
We can "put ourselves in their shoes."
We can "get inside their heads."
We can see things the way they see them.

**Empathy** is a great word.

People who are trustworthy and pleasant have LOTS of empathy.

They understand others' feelings.
They understand how others see things.
And so they try not to hurt others.
It's smart to have empathy.

Let's use **empathy** in a some sentences.

1. "Sue felt bad that Ricardo's dog died. She had lots of empathy for Ricardo."
2. "Rafael had empathy for Maria. He knew Maria was sad about moving away."
3. "Chris stole Chen-Ling's new cassette player. Chris didn't care how Chen-Ling felt. Chris had no ________ for Chen-Ling."

4. "Kevin had the measles. Rashid knew how Kevin felt, because Rashid just had measles himself. Rashid had a lot of ________ for Kevin."

Is empathy a good thing to have?

Yes _____ No _____

Should everyone try to have empathy for others?

Yes _____ No _____

Do you remember Tyler-the-liar-cheater-thief? Do you think Tyler had empathy for others?

Yes _____ No _____

Chapter

# 16

# Understanding Julio:

## Practicing Empathy

Shut your eyes and read the following story.

Oops! I guess that won't work.

Let's try this. Relax. Get comfortable. Imagine what's happening in the story about Julio. (Pronounced "HOO-lee-oh." It's a Spanish name.) Julio is from Mexico City. Imagine how Julio feels. Try to have empathy for Julio. Try to understand Julio.

> It was a warm day in May . . . The last school bell just rang . . . Julio was walking to the bike rack . . . His birthday was last month, April 25. His grandparents gave him a brand new 10-speed mountain bike . . . He loved his new bike . . . He was anxious to ride it home.
>
> Julio got to the bike rack and looked at his new bike . . . Tears came to his eyes . . . He could not believe what he saw . . . Someone had trashed his bike . . .The tires were flat . . . They had big cuts in them . . . The beautiful purple paint had deep

scratches . . . The spokes on the wheels were kicked and bent . . . The handle grips were sliced up too . . .

Julio pushed his bike home . . . He sobbed all the way . . . Why had someone done this to his beautiful new bike? . . .

1. How did Julio feel?

   ______________________________

2. How do you know he felt that way?

   ______________________________

3. Would you feel the same way?

   Yes _____ No _____

4. Was it fair to Julio to trash his new bike?

   Yes _____ No _____

5. Would you like YOUR new bike damaged like that?

   Yes _____ No _____

6. Imagine YOU were the person who damaged Julio's bike. If someone saw you do it, would they think you are a swell person?

   Yes _____ No _____

7. If your friends knew that YOU trashed Julio's bike, would they trust you more?

   Yes _____ No _____

8. Would they like you better?

   Yes _____ No _____

9. Would YOU ever do that to someone's bike?

   Yes _____ No _____

10. Were you able to have empathy for Julio?

    Yes _____ No _____

Chapter

# 17

# I Have Rights, You Have Rights, Everybody's Gotta Have Rights!

Do you know what "RIGHTS" are?
When we say "You have rights," it means that you deserve to be treated **fairly, honestly,** and **nicely.** That's all.

"RIGHTS" ARE VERY IMPORTANT!

Everyone has "rights."
Your parents (and step-parents) have "rights."
Your brothers and sisters (and step-brothers and step-sisters) have "rights."
Other children have "rights"—even children you don't know.
Your teachers, neighbors, store clerks, bus drivers, and school custodians have "rights," too.

Would you believe it? Even your pet dog, cat, canary, goldfish, gerbil, snake, and toad have rights.
They have a right to be cared for. They have a right not to be mistreated.

“We are your pets. Please respect our rights. Thank you.”

**“Respecting others' rights” just means treating people fairly, honestly, and nicely.**

**“Respecting others' rights” just means treating people the way YOU like to be treated.**

Let's use the word “rights” in some sentences. This will make the meaning more clear.

Big kids do not have the “right” to **hurt** you.
No one has the “right” to **hurt** you.
No one has the “right” to **steal** your things.
No one has the “right” to **damage** your things.
No one has the “right” to be **unfair** to you, to **cheat** you, to **lie** to you.

No one has the “_______” to make **messes**—then make you clean them up.
No one has the “_______” to be **cruel** to you.
No one has the “_______” to be **rude** to you.
No one has the “_______” to **touch** you where you don't want to be touched.

YOU do not have the “right” to **punch** little kids, just because you feel like doing it.

YOU do not have the "right" to **steal** someone's jacket, just because you want it.
YOU do not have the "right" to **damage** other people's things.
YOU do not have the "_______" to be **unfair** to others, or to **cheat** them, or to **lie** to them.
YOU do not have the "_______" to make others clean up your **messes**.
YOU do not have the "_______" to be **mean** or **rude** to others.

Your friends at school do not have the "right" to **snoop** through your locker.
YOU do not have the "_______" to **snoop** through your friends' things. Or your sister's things. Or your parent's things.

Your teacher has the "right" to be treated **nicely**.
You have the "right" to be treated **nicely** also.
Your friends have the "_______" to be treated **fairly**.
You have the "_______" to be treated **fairly** and **honestly**.

Do you understand what rights are?

Yes _____ No _____

Is respecting others' rights a good idea?

Yes _____ No _____

Chapter

# 18

# Rights Quiz:

## Can You Get the "Right" Answers?

Let's take a "Rights Quiz" to see if you understand others' rights and our own rights.

Check "True" or "False."

| | True | False |
|---|---|---|
| 1. Jason is bigger than Kristin. So Jason has the right to push Kristin around whenever he wants. | ☐ | ☐ |
| 2. Even if Kristin is small, she has the right NOT to be bullied. | ☐ | ☐ |
| 3. Jason stole your boom box. Jason respects your rights. | ☐ | ☐ |

| | True | False |
|---|---|---|
| 4. Jason does not have a boom box. So Jason has the right to steal yours. | ☐ | ☐ |
| 5. Juanita is from Puerto Rico. Terrell calls her names. He tells her to "Go back where you came from!" Terrell respects Juanita's rights. | ☐ | ☐ |
| 6. Juanita is a nice person, just like you. She has a right to be treated nicely. | ☐ | ☐ |
| 7. If Terrell is in a bad mood, he has the right to be rude and cruel to Juanita | ☐ | ☐ |
| 8. You are crabby. When your teacher asks you to do things, you pull faces and say "Oh crap!" You are showing respect for your teacher's right to be treated nicely. | ☐ | ☐ |
| 9. Shawana makes messes in the class. The teacher, custodian, or other students have to clean up her messes. Shawana has lots of respect for others' rights. | ☐ | ☐ |
| 10. Sarita lied to you. She said that "Our teacher doesn't like you." This hurt your feelings and made you feel very bad. Sarita has a right to lie to you and make you feel bad if she wants to. | ☐ | ☐ |
| 11. One day you were not home. Your big sister snooped through all of your drawers and boxes. She has a right to snoop through your things. | ☐ | ☐ |

| | True | False |
|---|---|---|
| 12. Lakesha was in a car accident. Now she must use a wheelchair. You tell your friends that "She's crippled! She doesn't belong in our class!" You are showing respect for Lakesha's right to be treated nicely and fairly. | ☐ | ☐ |
| 13. Nathan has trouble reading. Chelsea says, "Nathan's a dummy. He belongs in a school for dummies!" Chelsea is showing respect for Nathan's rights. | ☐ | ☐ |
| 14. One night, Jack, Tanya, Roberto, and Joel broke some school windows. They also spray painted the sidewalk. They had a right to do this because they don't like the principal. | ☐ | ☐ |
| 15. Your mom gets you off to school, then she goes to work. You try to help as much as you can. You believe your mom works hard and has a right to some help. | ☐ | ☐ |
| 16. Understanding your own rights and respecting other people's rights is a VERY good idea. | ☐ | ☐ |

Score: If you understand that YOU have rights and OTHERS have rights, you marked "True" to numbers 2, 6, 15, and 16. You marked "False" to all of the others (1, 3, 4, 5, 7, 8, 9, 10, 11, 12, 13, and 14).

How did you do? Do you understand your rights? Do you understand other people's rights?

AND . . . Check any items you missed. Maybe you did not understand the statement.

Chapter 19

# Rights and Values:

## A Crossword Puzzle

Have you ever worked a crossword puzzle?

They are fun—and challenging!

Write the answers or ideas in the "checkerboard." Put one letter in each square. Start each answer in the square that has the same number as the question.

Most of the words are related to values and rights. But some are not.

Write "Across" words in the regular way, from left to right.

Write "Down" words from top to bottom (vertically).

The answers are at the end of the book.

## Crossword Puzzle

ACROSS

1. Abbreviation for "Library."
4. The sound a hummingbird makes.
6. At the beginning of this book, we talked about big ________ and little ________ . (It means about the same thing as *choices.*)
8. We don't like to be __________, and so we should not __________ other people. (It rhymes with *flirt.*)
10. This word means about the same thing as *decisions.*
12. If you don't take care of your health, you may get _______. (It rhymes with *Bill.*)
13. What do we call people who are NOT nice when they talk to us? (It rhymes with *food.*)

14. If you try to understand how others feel, you have ________ for them.
18. Abraham Lincoln's nickname was "________ Abe."
19. We don't like it when others cheat at games. We all should play ________.
21. A good way to get arrested, spend time in juvenile detention centers, or get shot is to join a teenage ________.
23. Another good way to get arrested, spent time in juvenile detention centers, or get shot is to sell __________ . (Hint: You ruin your health if you use them.)
25. An important person, who can trash his/her life if he/she makes big mistakes; or who can live a pleasant and good life if he/she makes good choices and decisions. (It rhymes with *knee*.)
26. Albert's nickname.
27. The ________ most important words in this book are *values* and *empathy*. (Count 'em.)
28. The two most important words in this book are ________ and *empathy*.
29. Doctor: "Open your mouth and say ________."
31. We don't like it when others tell ________ to us. We like them to be honest and trustworthy. (It rhymes with *flies*.)
34. The opposite of "help." (It rhymes with *dirt*.)
35. Abbreviation for South Dakota.

DOWN

1. We make ________ decisions and we make big decisions.
3. We make little decisions and we make ________ decisions.
4. A two-letter word for "hello."
5. We don't like it when others leave a ________ for us to clean up.
7. We don't like it when others ________ into our personal stuff. (It rhymes with *droop*.)
8. Same as 8 Across.
9. Let's get ________ of bad values. (It rhymes with *Sid*.)
10. What do you call someone who cheats a lot? A ________.

11. A mouse catcher that purrs.
15. Pie with ice cream on it is called "Pie ________ mode." (Two words.)
16. Opposite of him.
17. Opposite of "No."
18. If we eat well, get exercise, and don't smoke, we are more likely to have good ________.
19. A _______ Newton is a cookie.
20. When we need help, we like people who ________ ________ (two words).
22. A person who is unpleasant, mean, and cranky is a _______. (It rhymes with *pouch*.)
23. David's nickname.
24. We don't like it when people ________ our things. (It rhymes with *real*.)
25. Opposite of "Pa."
29. What do these words have in common: Action, actor, actress, actual, activity, acting, actinium?
30. We should be fair to people at home and ________ school.
32. Being a "good person" ________ a good idea. (Rhymes with *Fizz*.)
33. Edward's nickname.

Chapter

# 20

# Julio the Custodian:

## More About Empathy, More About Rights

Empathy and rights are IMPORTANT to everyone, including YOU.

We need to think about how others feel.
We need to think about others' rights.
Why?
So that we will treat them like we want them to treat us.
Simple idea, isn't it?

Let's practice empathy some more. We can think about "rights" while we are at it?

Do you remember the story in Chapter 16 about Julio, whose bike was trashed? Imagine that Julio has grown up. He works as the custodian at your school.

Get comfortable. Imagine what's happening in the story. Especially, think about how Julio feels. Think about Julio's rights.

Julio has worked as the custodian at your school for five years . . . He makes sure that the bells work and the lights work . . . On cold days he makes sure that the furnace works . . . Each day after school, he makes sure that the rooms are swept clean . . . He empties trash cans . . . He cleans chalkboards . . . He varnishes the floors . . . Sometimes he paints the restrooms and the hallways . . . Julio likes his job. He is proud of his work . . . He tries to make the school a clean, comfortable, and pretty place for everyone.

One day after school, Julio went to clean the restrooms . . . He had just painted them . . . He found that somebody had scratched some swear words on the walls . . . They drew some pictures, too . . . A light was broken . . . Toilet paper was all over the floor . . . A soap dispenser was smashed . . .

Julio didn't cry. He was too old for that . . . But he felt very bad just the same.

"Now I have to do a lot more work," thought Julio . . . "I will have to sandpaper the scratches and paint the wall again . . . I will have to clean up the paper . . . I will have to put in a new soap dispenser . . . I wish that person would not have done this . . . I have other work to do . . . It costs money to fix things that children break . . .

Let's think about "pretty" ☺ and "ugly." ☹
Let's think about *fairness.* ☺
Let's think about *people's rights.* ☺
Let's think about *empathy.* ☺
Let's think about *the kind of person YOU want to be.* ☺

| | **Yes** | **No** |
|---|---|---|
| 1. Do you like ugly restrooms better than nice neat ones? | ☐ | ☐ |
| 2. Do restrooms look prettier when people damage them? | ☐ | ☐ |
| 3. Do thoughtful people with good values trash restrooms? | ☐ | ☐ |
| 4. Was it fair to make Julio do extra work? | ☐ | ☐ |
| 5. Did the person who did this damage think about Julio's FEELINGS? | ☐ | ☐ |
| 6. Did the person who did this damage think about Julio's RIGHTS? | ☐ | ☐ |

**Empathy exercise**: Write about how Julio felt when he found the mess in the restroom.

______________________________________________________________________

______________________________________________________________________

______________________________________________________________________

______________________________________________________________________

______________________________________________________________________

______________________________________________________________________

Chapter

# 21

# Is Stealing Wrong

## (Because You Might Get Caught)?

---

Let's think about *empathy*.
A newspaper reporter told this story.
He asked some teenagers:

> **"Why is it wrong to steal from other students?"**

Here is what they said:

> "Because the other students might find out."
> "Because I might get caught."
> "Because I might get into trouble."

NOT ONE STUDENT thought about the other students' rights.
NOT ONE STUDENT thought about the other students' feelings.
NOT ONE STUDENT thought about good values and bad values.
NOT ONE STUDENT said:

> "Because the other students would feel bad."
> "Because I know how they would feel."

"Because I would not like MY things stolen."
"Because I don't have the right to steal other people's things."

**These teenagers did not try to understand how others felt when their things were stolen. They did not have EMPATHY for other students. All they could think about was, "Gee whiz, *I* might get caught! *I* might get into trouble!" They just thought about THEMSELVES.**

Should we think about other people's rights and feelings?

Yes ____ No ____

Will YOU will think about other people's rights?

Yes ____ No ____

Will YOU think about other people's feelings?

Yes ____ No ____

Are YOU able to have empathy?

Yes ____ No ____

Terrific! You probably already have GREAT values! ☺

☆☆☆☆☆☆☆☆☆☆☆☆☆☆☆☆☆☆☆☆☆

*Award for Outstanding Values*

*Your name* ______________________________

☆☆☆☆☆☆☆☆☆☆☆☆☆☆☆☆☆☆☆☆☆

Chapter

# 22

# The Simpson Case, Part I:

## Mystery at King Elementary

Ms. Marta Clark is the principal of King Elementary School. When she arrived on Monday morning, she got a big, sad surprise. The secretaries were surprised and sad too. And so were all the teachers. The custodian shook his head and said, "Oh no, more work!" When the children arrived, nearly all of them felt very bad.

The entrance to their pretty school was a mess. White, black, and green paint was sloshed all over the doors. It dripped on the sidewalk. It spilled under the door into the hallway. Some of the little windows in the door were broken. Some classroom windows were broken too.

Mr. Lang arrived soon. He was a police detective. He looked at the paint. He looked at the doors. He looked all around the crime scene. He found a glove with black, white, and green paint on it. He found three empty paint cans behind some bushes. They were in a brown paper sack. A store receipt was also in the sack.

The receipt said "3 Cans of Paint $6.25." The receipt also said "Handy Harry's Hardware." The date on the receipt was just last Saturday.

Mr. Lang went to the Handy Harry's Hardware store. The owner, Handy Harry, said "Yes, I was working on Saturday. I sold the paint to Jay Simpson."

Mr. Lang went to Jay's home. He saw Jay's bike leaning against a tree. The bike had drops of black, white, and green paint on it. He found the other glove. It had paint on it too. He went back to school and told Ms. Clark, the Principal, what he had found.

Jay lives with his grandmother, Mrs. Simpson. Ms. Clark telephoned Jay's grandmother. Ms. Clark told Mrs. Simpson what had happened and what Detective Lang had found. She asked Jay's grandmother, "Please come to school, Mrs. Simpson. I must talk with you."

Jay was sitting in Ms. Clark's office when his grandmother arrived. Mrs. Simpson brought her brother, Johnny Coffman. Mr. Coffman was a lawyer.

Before Ms. Clark could say a word, Johnny Coffman said, "This boy is innocent! He didn't do anything."

Ms. Clark was surprised. She said, "But Handy Harry sold that paint to Jay on Saturday. Detective Lang found paint on Jay's bicycle. I think Jay did it." She turned to Jay, "Did you do it Jay?"

"Don't say a word!" said Mr. Coffman. "You didn't do it. Somebody else put that paint on your bike. Somebody else is trying to blame you!"

Then Mr. Coffman turned to Ms. Clark. "Jay was framed! He would not buy some drugs. So the drug dealer trashed the school. The drug dealer put the drops of paint on Jay's bicycle. He put the painty glove there, too!"

Ms. Clark said, "But Handy Harry sold him the paint and ... "

"Nonsense," said Mr. Coffman. "Can he prove it? Does he have a photo of Jay buying the paint? He made a mistake. Somebody else bought the paint. One of those drug dealers bought the paint."

Just then, two people walked into the office. One was Rosy Lopez. She said, "Ms. Clark, I was walking past the school on Saturday evening. I saw Jay throw the paint and break the windows."

The other person was Mr. Handy from the hardware store. He said, "Ms. Clark, I have a video picture of Jay buying the paint. He bought the paint for sure."

Then Ms. Clark looked at Jay's shoes. "Jay," she said, "you have paint on the side of your shoe."

Jay looked at the floor. He was very upset. "Okay," he said. "I did it. I'm sorry. I thought it would be fun. But I really messed up the school. I wish I hadn't done it. I'm sorry. I REALLY wish I hadn't done it."

Johnny Coffman, the lawyer, looked at Jay. Then he left without saying a word.

Jay's grandmother's eyes turned red and she began to sob. "What will happen now?"

Ms. Clark said, "I will have to turn this over to the juvenile authorities. They will decide. He might be placed in a juvenile detention home for a while. You will have to pay for the damage. It might cost a thousand dollars. I hope Jay learned a lesson from this."

Chapter

# 23

# The Simpson Case, Part II:

## Lessons To Learn

There are lots of lessons about VALUES in the Simpson Case.

Based on what you know about:

- Good and bad values
- Others' feelings
- Others' rights
- Empathy
- Respect

Answer "Yes" or "No" to each question:

| | Yes | No |
|---|---|---|
| 1. Did Jay have the right to trash the school? | ☐ | ☐ |
| 2. Do other children at King Elementary have the right to a pretty school? | ☐ | ☐ |
| 3. Did Jay think about the rights and feelings of other students? | ☐ | ☐ |
| 4. Did Jay think about the rights of the custodian? | ☐ | ☐ |
| 5. SHOULD Jay think about other people's rights? | ☐ | ☐ |
| 6. Did Jay think about how Ms. Clark would feel? Or how the custodian would feel? | ☐ | ☐ |
| 7. Did Jay think about how his grandmother would feel when she found out? | ☐ | ☐ |
| 8. Did Jay "put himself in the shoes" of the custodian, the other students, his grandmother, or Ms. Clark? | ☐ | ☐ |
| 9. Should Jay have empathy for others? | ☐ | ☐ |
| 10. Will Jay's grandmother really, really enjoy paying $1,000 for Jay's damage? | ☐ | ☐ |
| 11. Did Jay feel really, really GOOD in the principal's office? | ☐ | ☐ |
| 12. Was Jay PROUD of himself? Did he have lots of SELF-RESPECT? | ☐ | ☐ |

| | Yes | No |
|---|---|---|
| 13. Will the other students think Jay is a really swell person? Will they have more RESPECT for Jay? | ☐ | ☐ |
| 14. Or will they think Jay is a JERK? | ☐ | ☐ |
| 15. Will Ms. Clark and Jay's teachers have more RESPECT for Jay? | ☐ | ☐ |
| 16. Did the damage make the school look pretty? | ☐ | ☐ |
| 17. Did the damage make the school look ugly? | ☐ | ☐ |
| 18. Did Jay make a GOOD DECISION when trashed the school? | ☐ | ☐ |
| 19. Did Jay THINK about how his ACTIONS would have bad CONSEQUENCES? | ☐ | ☐ |
| 20. Do people with good values destroy other people's property? | ☐ | ☐ |
| 21. Would YOU ignore other people's rights and trash their property? | ☐ | ☐ |

Chapter

# 24

# You Don't Need a Friend Like Kate!:

## Returning Things, Keeping Promises, Trustworthiness, and Promptness

---

This is a story about you and your friend Kate.

Relax, shut your eyes, and read the story. Oops, I forgot again!

Well, read the story with your eyes open. Imagine what is happening. Imagine your feelings. Think about what is right and what is wrong.

> You are waiting for your friend Kate in front of the school . . . The time is 3:45 p.m. Kate promised to be there (for sure!) at 3:30 . . . You are not surprised she is late. Kate forgets her promises all the time . . . Today she was supposed to return your cassettes . . . You wonder if you will ever see them again . . . Kate doesn't return things either . . . Finally, you give up and go home . . .
>
> At eight o'clock that evening Kate calls. She asks, "Can I borrow your calculator for a class project? . . . You think about it for a minute, then say, "Sure, I'll bring it to school tomorrow." Then you ask, "Where were you today, Kate. I waited for half an hour?" . . . Kate says, "Well, I went to the hobby store with Fred. We needed some colored paper. Meet me tomorrow at 3:30—I promise I'll be there . . . Oh, I had a

little problem with one of your cassettes. It fell in some mud. But I think it still sounds all right, sort of . . . It wasn't my fault" . . . "Sure Kate," you say. "That's okay. I'll see you tomorrow" . . .

Should Kate have met you when she said she would?

Yes _____ No _____

Is it important to keep promises?

Yes _____ No _____

Is it all right to keep people waiting like Kate did?

Yes _____ No _____

It is all right to borrow things and not return them?

Yes _____ No _____

When you borrow things, is it all right to wreck them?

Yes _____ No _____

How do you FEEL when people don't return your things? Or they return them broken?

_______________________________________________

Why is it important to return things promptly, and not broken?

_______________________________________________

Is your friend Kate trustworthy?

Yes _____ No _____

Would you like a lot of friends like Kate?

Yes _____ No _____

Should YOU be like Kate?

Yes ______ No _____

Chapter

# A Funny Thing Happened in the Classroom Today:

## Thinking About Rights of Teachers

---

Let's read another story that you can imagine in your "mind's eye."

YOU are going to be the teacher!

Imagine your feelings.

Think about your rights.

Think about students showing respect.

Imagine that YOU are a new fifth-grade teacher . . . You are at the chalk board trying to explain how to add 1/2 plus 1/4 . . . Nobody is paying any attention AT ALL! . . . Juan is scratching a sore on his ankle . . . Shaneka is reading a comic book . . . Ling-Jen is writing a note to Jenny . . . She passes the note . . . Jenny reads it and giggles . . . Jenny wads up the note and throws it at the wastebasket . . . Kevin is at the back of the room folding airplanes . . . He has about 30 so far . . .

Bill, Carlos, and Leon are whispering about a new Batman movie . . . Then Greg walks into class late, and sits down wearing earphones.

You say, "Greg, please take off the earphones. Music time is not until 2:30" . . . Greg does nothing—because he can't hear you.

Then you ask Ling-Jen, "How can we add 1/2 plus 1/4?" . . . Ling-Jen is startled. She drops the pencil she was writing another note with . . . She answers, "How can we who?" . . . Kevin sails a couple of airplanes . . . Everyone giggles . . . You ask, "Who can solve this problem?" . . . No one knows what you are talking about . . . Everyone looks at you and says, "Huh? What problem?"

Remember, YOU are the teacher.

How do you feel when nobody pays attention?

______________________________________________________________

Are your students respecting your rights?

Yes _____ No _____

Are you being treated fairly or badly?

Fairly _____ Badly _____

Do you have a right to be listened to?

Yes _____ No _____

While you are trying to teach, do students have the RIGHT to read comic books? Write notes to each other? Sail airplanes? Talk about movies? Walk in late? Wear earphones?

Yes _____ No _____

Teachers try hard to do a good job. Do they deserve respect?

Yes _____ No _____

Chapter

# Self-Control:

## A Tale About Willy-the-Wild

"Self-control" means what it says.

It means that you "control yourself."

You control your actions.

You think about consequences.

**Scene: Somewhere in your town, near a rose bush. Willy-the-Wild is yelling at his friends, Nateesha and Carlos.**

Wild Willy: (Screaming) I got a thorn in my toe! IT HURTS! You guys put it there! You're REAL JERKS! Don't leave your thorns lying around! IT'S ALL YOUR FAULT!

Nateesha: But Willy, that's not our thorn. You walked through those rose bushes!

Wild Willy: (Still screaming) Well, people shouldn't leave their rose bushes lying around where I want to walk! Some people are REAL JERKS! This wasn't MY fault. I'm going to GET somebody for this!

Carlos: Hey, take it easy, Willy! It was an accident. Relax. I'll pull out the thorn! No problem!

Nateesha: And Willy, please work on your self-control!

Should Willy-The-Wild yell at everybody, blame them, and threaten them?

Yes _____ No _____

Should Willy use self-control?

Yes _____ No _____

Is it a "good decision" to yell at people when you are angry?

Yes _____ No _____

Is it a "good decision" to blame people and threaten them when you are angry?

Yes _____ No _____

If you were Willy, would YOU have better self-control?

Yes _____ No _____

Chapter

# 27

# A Sad-But-True Story About Self-Control

This is a true story.

It happened in Milwaukee, Wisconsin, a few weeks before I wrote this chapter.

Some people were playing basketball on a public basketball court. A man about 29 years old got mad at a nine-year old boy. Maybe the boy said something rude. Maybe he swore at the man. We don't know. *The man went to his car and got a gun. He came back and shot the boy in the head.* The boy is dead. The man was sent to prison for 30 years.

Did the man show GOOD SELF-CONTROL when he got angry?

Yes _____ No _____

Did the man make a GOOD DECISION?

Yes _____ No _____

Did the man THINK about the consequences of his actions?

Yes _____ No _____

Did the man THINK about what a terrible, terrible thing he was doing?

Yes _____ No _____

Did the man THINK about what was best for the boy?

Yes _____ No _____

Did the man THINK about what was best for himself?

Yes _____ No _____

Did the man THINK about how the boy's mother and father would feel?

Yes _____ No _____

Did the man THINK about how his own family would feel?

Yes _____ No _____

How do you think the boy's family felt? Happy? Terribly sad?

_______________________________________________

How do you think the man's family felt? Happy? Terribly sad?

_______________________________________________

Would YOU get mad and SHOOT somebody because of an argument in a basketball game?

Yes _____ No _____

When you are angry at someone, is it really, really, important to YELL at them or HURT them?

Yes _____ No _____

Is it better to use self-control when you feel upset or angry?

Yes _____ No _____

❀❀❀❀❀❀❀❀❀❀

Here are some things you can do when you are angry:

Check the ones that you think are BETTER than shooting somebody.

_____Talk to a friend.

_____Talk to the person you are angry at.

_____Change your mood by exercise or some other physical activity. (Jogging is good.)

_____Find something else to do, something you enjoy. Maybe play a game.

What else can you do to make yourself feel better?

______________________________________________

______________________________________________

**ANYTHING is better than shooting somebody.**

**ANYTHING is better than destroying their life and your own.**

Chapter

# 28

# Different Values for Different Folks:

## Family? Helping Others? Sports? Money? Looking Nice?

In Chapter 3 we talked about why VALUES are so IMPORTANT.

### OUR VALUES . . .

- ➔ Are our own ideas about what is RIGHT and what is WRONG.
- ➔ Are part of WHO we are.
- ➔ Are OUR OWN RULES that we live by.
- ➔ Guide our DECISIONS and what we DO.
- ➔ Affect our FEELINGS about others and ourselves.
- ➔ Determine how GOOD our LIVES will become.
- ➔ Guide us in making little decisions and BIG decisions.

All of us have LOTS of values.

And different people will have different values.

These are some things that different people value most:

| | |
|---|---|
| A good education | Sports |
| Looking extra nice | Being friendly and helping others |
| Fun and pleasure | Good manners |
| One's family | Money |
| Being honest and trustworthy | Music |
| Taking care of the environment | Having friends and belonging to groups |

Read each statement. Write down which of these values is most important to each person? (The answers are at the end of this chapter.)

1. Lavonzelle spends a lot of time playing computer games. She also goes to the ice cream store and watches TV. Lavonzelle likes having a good time. Lavonzelle seems to value ________________.

2. Jeffrey spends a lot of money on nice clothes. His hair is always just right. Jeffrey seems to value ________________.

3. Mohammed is honest and keeps his promises. He never cheats at anything. Mohammed seems to value ________________.

4. Yolanda works hard in school. She plans to go to college. Yolanda values ________________.

5. Kai-Shun plays little league softball on Tuesdays. He plays soccer on Wednesdays. He takes swimming lessons every Saturday. He plays basketball after school whenever he can. He also goes fishing. Kai-Shun values __________________.

6. Manuel helps take care of his little sister. He likes to visit relatives. He likes to go places and do things with his mom, dad, and little sister. Manuel values his __________________.

7. Denzel dropped off the soccer team so he could get a part-time job. He likes to be able to buy things. Denzel seems to value __________________.

8. Chantal likes to play the piano. She also plays the French horn. She likes to go to concerts. Chantal values __________________.

9. Donna enjoys helping the neighbors. She waters plants and brings in mail. She cares for animals when neighbors are on trips. She asks the teacher if she can help with anything. Donna seems to value __________________.

10. Jocelyn picks up trash as she walks to school. She likes to help her mom recycle things. She enjoys forests and nature. She likes to help keep her world beautiful. Jocelyn values __________________.

11. Maria likes to be around people. She has lots of friends. She joins lots of after-schools clubs. Maria values __________________.

12. Prince enjoys opening doors for people. He always sends "Thank You" notes to people who give him birthday presents. He is a pleasant and polite person. Prince values __________________.

Can a person have LOTS of GOOD values?

Yes _____ No _____

What do YOU value?

What is important to YOU?

Check ✔ the blank that shows how much you value each item.

| | Not at All | A Little | More Than a Little | A Lot |
|---|---|---|---|---|
| A Good Education | ___ | ___ | ___ | ___ |
| Sports | ___ | ___ | ___ | ___ |
| Looking extra nice | ___ | ___ | ___ | ___ |
| Being friendly and helping others | ___ | ___ | ___ | ___ |
| Fun and pleasure | ___ | ___ | ___ | ___ |
| One's family | ___ | ___ | ___ | ___ |
| Good manners | ___ | ___ | ___ | ___ |
| Being honest and trustworthy | ___ | ___ | ___ | ___ |
| Money | ___ | ___ | ___ | ___ |
| Music | ___ | ___ | ___ | ___ |
| Taking care of the environment | ___ | ___ | ___ | ___ |
| Having friends and belonging to groups | ___ | ___ | ___ | ___ |

What else do you value?

______________________________________________

______________________________________________

______________________________________________

Answers: 1. Lavonzelle values fun and pleasure. 2. Jeffrey values looking extra nice. 3. Mohammed values being honest (and trustworthy). 4. Yolanda values a good education. 5. Kai-Shun values sports. 6. Manuel values his family. 7. Denzel values money. 8. Chantal values music. 9. Donna values helping others. 10. Jocelyn values taking care of the environment. 11. Maria values having friends and belonging to groups. 12. Prince values good manners.

# Some People Prefer Hurtful Values:

## Making Bad Decisions, Making Bad Choices

---

In the last chapter, we learned that different people value different things.

All of those values were pretty good ones. We talked about values like helping others, education, money, looking nice, being honest, good manners, sports, music, and having friends.

But some people have a lot of *bad* values, values that can hurt others or hurt ourselves.

Some bad values are:

a. Being rude; not being polite
b. Not respecting others' rights; hurting others; damaging others' property
c. Stealing; being a criminal
d. Cheating; being unfair
e. Making people afraid of you; being a "tough guy"; being a bully
f. Dropping out of school (not getting an education and training)
g. Dumping garbage wherever you want; leaving messes
h. Criticizing or being rude to people with disabilities, elderly people
i. Ignoring safety rules

Here is a quiz.

**Which of the values in the box seems most important to each person?**

Just write the letter (a, b, c, etc.) of the values in the above list.

You can use the same letter more than once.

The answers are at the end of this chapter.

1. Ernesto tosses stuff AT trash cans—but he doesn't care if he misses. After he eats his burger and fries, he throws the wrappers any place he wants—but NOT in trash cans.

   Ernesto values: _____.

Some bad values are:

a. Being rude; not being polite

b. Not respecting others' rights; hurting others; damaging others' property

c. Stealing; being a criminal

d. Cheating; being unfair

e. Making people afraid of you; being a "tough guy"; being a bully

f. Dropping out of school (not getting an education and training)

g. Dumping garbage wherever you want; leaving messes

h. Criticizing or being rude to people with disabilities, elderly people

i. Ignoring safety rules

2. Dayvene thinks safety rules are for sissies. She runs in the halls. She slides down bannisters. She ignores fire drills (as long as she can). She tilts her chair back until it falls over. She plays with electrical wires. She practices tightrope walking on the tops of fences.

   Dayvene values: _____.

3. Jarvell shoves little kids out of the way. He slaps his little sister. He tells people to "Shut up!"

   Jarvell values: _____.

4. Jennifer never says "Thanks." She never holds the door open for anyone. At the table, she says "Gimme the butter!" instead of "Please pass the butter." She also tells people "Oh, shut up!" Jennifer is never polite to anyone.

Jennifer values: _____.

5. William yells at old people from his bicycle ("Hey Granny, where's your rocker?"). He is mean to students with disabilities ("Hey Nancy, get outta' that wheelchair! You just want attention!" "Hey Fred, why can't ya read? Are you a dummy or what?" "Hi, Scar-face!").

   William values: _____.

6. Lavonna doesn't like school work. She wants to quit school as soon as she can.

   Lavonna values: _____.

7. Ray wants to join a gang. He wants to get a gun. He wants to push people around and threaten them.

   Ray values: _____.

8. Nathan cheats at games and cheats on tests. He always wants to be first for everything. At home, he doesn't give his sister a fair share of anything—he always wants the most.

   Nathan values: _____.

9. Oleka talks mean to her parents. She yells at people who get in her way. Sometimes, she is not polite to her teacher. Oleka values: _____.

10. Jack is a thief. If something fits in his pocket, he'll steal it. When he grows up, he wants to be a burglar.

    Jack values: _____.

11. Maria scratches pictures on restroom walls and bus stops. Sometimes she breaks car windows just for fun.

    Maria values: _____.

Can one person have LOTS of bad, hurtful values?

Yes _____ No _____

Should EVERYONE have bad, hurtful values?

Yes _____ No _____

Do YOU have bad, hurtful values?

Yes _____ No _____

Answers:

1. g (Ernesto)
2. i (Dayvene)
3. e (or a or b) (Jarvell)
4. a (Jennifer)
5. h (William)
6. f (Lavonna)
7. e (Ray)
8. d (Nathan)
9. a (Oleka)
10. c (Jack)
11. b (Maria)

Chapter

# 30

# "What Would Happen If . . .

## We Do EXTRA Nice Things for People?"

Do you remember our "What would happen if . . . ?" problem? ("What would happen if everyone were like Tyler?" Tyler was a thief, vandal, cheater, liar—the works!)

Let's think about this problem: "What would happen if . . . ?" we did a lot of EXTRA nice things for people.

How would people feel?

What would they think about us?

What would they say?

**What would happen if . . . you started to help with dishes without being asked?**

Mom (or other adult) would feel ________________________.

She (or he) would think that you are ____________________.

She (or he) probably would say, "______________________."

**What would happen if . . . you volunteered to help your teacher erase the board after school?**

She (or he) would feel

________________________________.

She (or he) would think that you are

___________________.

She (or he) probably would say,

"______________________."

**What would happen if . . . you were EXTRA nice to a new student in your class?**

She (or he) would feel ______________________________.

She (or he) would think that you are ____________________.

She (or he) probably would say, "______________________."

**What would happen if . . . you found a purse—with $100 in it? The lady's name and address were in the purse, and you returned it to her.**

She would feel ____________________________________.

She would think that you are __________________________.

She probably would say, "____________________________."

(And she probably would give you a nice reward!)

**Lashay is in a wheelchair in your class. Not many people talk to her. What would happen if . . . you were EXTRA nice to Lashay? You say "Good morning, how are you today, Lashay?" And you give her compliments on her clothes and her good school work.**

Lashay would feel ______________________________.

She would think that you are __________________________.

She probably would say, "____________________________."

**Imagine that your family has a dog or a cat named "Clinton." (Maybe you DO have a dog or cat.) What would happen if . . . you help take EXTRA good care of Clinton.**

Clinton would feel

______________________________.

Clinton would think that you are

____________________.

If Clinton could talk, he probably would say,

"________________________________________."

❀❀❀❀❀❀❀❀❀❀

When people are EXTRA nice to you . . .

How do you FEEL? ______________________________.

What do you THINK of them? ________________________.

What might you SAY to them? "________________________."

Chapter

# 31

# Word Search for Friendly, Caring Words

Let's do another word search puzzle.

**Friendly, caring** words are hidden in the block of letters.

The words are printed left to right or top to bottom. Two words are printed backwards—right to left.

Find the following words and draw a ring around them

| | | |
|---|---|---|
| Agreeable | Helpful | Caring |
| I Like You | Cheery | Kind |
| Courteous | Nice | Friends |
| Pleasant | Go For It | Smiling |

The solution is at the end of the book.

Chapter 32

# Word Search for Rude, Hurtful Words

One more word search.

This time, let's find **rude, hurtful** words.

Words that we DON'T like people to say TO us.

Words that we DON'T like people to say ABOUT us.

The words can be printed left to right or top to bottom. One word is printed backwards—right to left.

Find the words and draw a ring around them

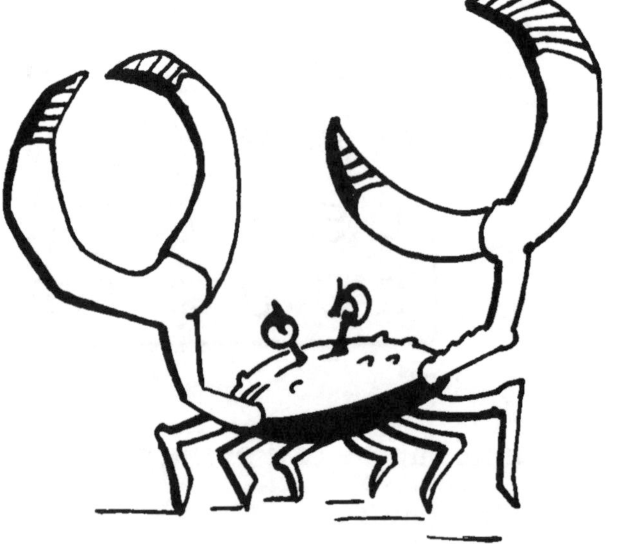

| | | |
|---|---|---|
| Angry | Go Away | Creep |
| Idiot | Dope | I Hate You |
| Drop Dead | Jerk | Dummy |
| Nerd | Get Lost | Shut Up |

| | | | | | | | | | |
|---|---|---|---|---|---|---|---|---|---|
| D | R | O | P | D | E | A | D | X | G |
| Z | Y | N | S | H | U | T | U | P | O |
| K | R | E | J | A | B | D | M | W | A |
| H | G | R | O | Q | Z | C | M | F | W |
| I | V | D | A | N | G | R | Y | L | A |
| D | W | X | Q | P | U | E | D | Q | Y |
| I | Z | I | H | A | T | E | Y | O | U |
| O | D | O | P | E | R | P | E | M | X |
| T | J | G | E | T | L | O | S | T | K |

The solution is at the end of the book.

Chapter

# 33

# Imagine You Work at Burger Queen:

## Behaving Badly in Public

---

CONGRATULATIONS! You just got a job at Burger Queen!

Relax. Imagine what is happening as you read this story.

(Hint: It's about rudeness. It's about mistreating people who work in restaurants and stores. It's about behaving badly in public.)

Imagine that YOU have a job at Burger Queen . . . Burger Queen is the best fast-food restaurant in town . . . You like talking to people and cooking french fries . . . But some days, it seems like EVERYONE is pushy and rude . . .

One day, you are counting change for a little girl . . . A loud lady steps in front of the girl and says, "I want some ketchup! I want it right now! I'm in a hurry!" . . . Then a man yells at you, "Why don't you have any newspapers? . . . Don't you know how to run a Burger Queen?" . . . Two teenagers

walk up and say, "We want $10 worth of quarters for the video games next door" . . . You tell them, "I'm sorry, but we are almost out of quarters". . . They look at you and yell, "You're a stupid liar!" . . . A young woman walks up and says, "I want to cash this check for $200" . . . But you are not allowed to cash checks . . . She gets mad, too. She yells "You're a jerk! I'm never coming back here again!" . . .

Three high school students, two boys and a girl, are sitting in a booth . . . They are drawing pictures on their table with mustard . . . Their cups of soda and ice cubes fall to the floor . . . You know that you will have to clean up their mess . . .

How do you feel about all of this bad behavior?

_______________________________________________

Do you feel you deserve respect?

Yes _____ No _____

Do you have the right to be treated nicely?

Yes _____ No _____

Think about the rude, pushy people in this story.

Are they thinking of your FEELINGS?

Yes _____ No _____

Are they thinking of your RIGHTS?

Yes _____ No _____

Are they pleasant people?

Yes _____ No _____

Should YOU be like these people?

Yes _____ No _____

Chapter

# 34

# A Down Day, An Up Day:

## Friendliness, Helping Others, Valuing Friends

---

Imagine that your name is Chris . . . Your day has started badly . . . You are a little sick . . . Maybe it's the pizza, chop suey, and strawberry ice cream you ate last night . . . This morning you couldn't find two socks the same color . . . Oh well, green and purple look nice together . . . Your favorite blue sweater has some new moth holes in it, so you put on an old sweater . . . You wish your sister would get rid of her pet moths . . . At school you slip on the lawn . . . You get a big green grass stain on your tan pants . . . It look's just great! . . . Then you remember that you left your math homework home . . . It was due today! . . . And your mother fixed you a SPINACH sandwich for lunch . . . You are NOT in a real happy mood . . .

Then Tawana comes over and says "You look a bit down in the mouth, Chris, cheer up. Come on over after school. We'll listen to some tapes" . . . You smile and say "Okay" . . . You explain to your teacher that you forgot the math assignment . . . The teacher smiles and says, "Gee whiz, I've never forgotten anything in my life! Bring it in tomorrow, air head!" . . . You're beginning to feel a lot better! . . . After you sit down, Jan says "Say, that's a good looking sweater . . . I like it better than your blue one!" . . . Miguel smiles and says, "Hi Chris, have some peanuts! That's a nice looking grass stain" . . . You say, "Thanks. My mom's going to like it, too" . . . Somehow, your troubles don't seem so bad any more. . . .

♥♥♥♥♥♥♥♥♥♥♥♥♥

How do you feel when people are smiling, helpful, and friendly?

______________________________________________

How do you feel when people are grouchy and unpleasant?

______________________________________________

Do you LIKE people who are friendly and helpful?

Yes _____ No _____

Do you LIKE people who are grouchy and unpleasant?

Yes _____ No _____

Should we try to smile, be friendly, and help others?

Yes _____ No _____

Are good friends important?

Yes _____ No _____

Why are good friends important?

______________________________________________

Should YOU try to be a good friend?

Yes _____ No _____

♥♥♥♥♥♥♥♥♥♥♥♥♥

Chapter

# 35

# Empathy for the Elderly:

## A Story About Not Having Any!

This is an empathy exercise. It is based on a TRUE story.

Imagine you are an elderly person. Maybe 86 years old. As you read the story, imagine your thoughts and feelings.

YOU are an elderly man, a senior citizen . . . You live in a small home with your wife . . . One evening there is a knock on your door . . . You open the door and two young men burst in . . . One of them pushes you to the floor . . . You look up and see that he has a gun . . . How do you feel? . . . What do you think about?. . . He tells you he wants all of your money . . . All of your credit cards . . . Your wedding rings . . . All of your jewelry . . . Your cameras . . . Your radios . . . Your small color TV set . . . You tell him, "I have no money, it's all in the bank" . . . He hits you very hard with his pistol . . . You find yourself on the floor again . . . Your head hurts . . . You feel blood trickling down your forehead . . .

✳✳✳✳✳✳✳✳✳✳

Do you feel happy?

Yes _____ No _____

Do you feel frightened and worried?

Yes _____ No _____

What are you thinking about while you are being robbed?

_______________________________________________

✳✳✳✳✳✳✳✳✳✳

Now you are back in your own shoes.

Is it all right to rob and beat elderly people?

Yes _____ No _____

Does it really happen?

Yes _____ No _____

Who does this sort of thing?

Check which answers are correct?

____ Thoughtful people

____ Kind people

____ Honest people

____ Friendly people

____ People who have empathy for others

____ Intelligent people

I HOPE YOU DID NOT CHECK ANY OF THESE!

What do YOU think of people who do this?

______________________________________________________________

Do such criminals think about the RIGHTS of their victims?

Yes _____ No _____

Do such criminals think about the FEELINGS of their victims?

Yes _____ No _____

Do such criminals have a RIGHT to rob and beat people?

Yes _____ No _____

Would YOU ever do this?

Yes _____ No _____

Not many people would.

Chapter

# 36

# A Story About Larry:

## "What a Nice Guy!"

---

In the last chapter, you read a true story about young thieves. They robbed and beat some elderly people.

This story is about a jerk named Larry. The story is kind of true. (I knew some kids like Larry when I was in school.)

Get comfortable. As you read the story, imagine what is happening. Imagine how each person feels. Imagine what each person might be thinking.

> You are walking down the school hall . . . A big dumb guy named Larry looks at YOU . . . He yells, "Hey stupid, is that your face or a pile of garbage?" . . . Larry laughs . . . You are surprised and a little upset . . . You wonder why he talks like that . . . You think to yourself, "He's not a very nice person, he's rude!" . . .

In class, your teacher, Ms. Martinez, asks YOU "Which planet is closest to the sun?" . . . You think for a minute and then say "I don't remember" . . . Larry laughs out loud . . . He says, "That jerk don't know nothin' . . . Hey Martinez, ain't it time fer art yet?" . . . Ms. Martinez says, "My name is Ms. Martinez, and it's not time for art yet . . . And you tell me, Larry, which planet is the third planet from the sun?" . . . Larry says, "Huh? How should I know? I ain't never been there!" . . . Larry turns to Raynea in the next seat, "Hey toothpick, how come you're so tall an' skinny? Weather okay up there? Glad I ain't no toothpick" . . .

Finally it's art time . . . Larry walks to the front of the room . . . He picks out the best set of water colors . . . It has Raynea's name on it . . . Ms. Martinez sees Larry take Raynea's paints . . . She says, "Larry, if you want a different set of paints, please try asking" . . . Larry mumbles, "Uh, but I need this one . . . That toothpick don't need it" . . . After school, Larry looks at Ching Ping and laughs, "Hey, you're as ugly as a horse!"

☹☹☹☹☹☹☹☹☹☹☹

Do you like to have people yell at you?

Yes _____ No _____

Do you like to have people insult you?

Yes _____ No _____

Do you like it when people are rude to you?

Yes _____ No _____

Do you like people to call you names?

Yes _____ No _____

Does Larry have **empathy**? (Does he understand how people FEEL when he yells at them? Insults them? Treats them rudely? Calls them names?)

Yes _____ No _____

Are people like Larry considerate?

Yes _____ No _____

Thoughtful?

Yes _____ No _____

Intelligent?

Yes _____ No _____

Could YOU be like Larry?

**NO!** ☹☹☹

Chapter

# 37

# Crossword Puzzle:

## Your Basic Good Values

Let's review some of what we have learned so far.

We have ONE LAST CROSSWORD PUZZLE.

ACROSS

5. If we value *helpfulness*, we will ________ people.

7. It is good to have empathy. That is, it is good to try to ________ other people's feelings.

11. M-I-C-K-E-Y M-__-__-__-__.

12. Bad values hurt others and hurt us, ________ values help others and help us.

13. Remember, our ________ have consequences.

16. Are GOOD VALUES a good idea—for YOU and for your FUTURE LIFE?

18. If we want people to know that we are trustworthy, we should not cheat, steal, or ________ lies.

19. Arnold Schwarzenegger's initials.

21. ________ is not a good idea to drop out of school. (Rhymes with *fit, mitt,* and *nit-wit.*)

22. ________ are our ideas about what is RIGHT and what is WRONG.

    They are part of WHO we are.

    They are OUR OWN RULES that we live by.

    They guide our decisions and our behavior.

    They affect our FEELINGS about others and ourselves.

    They determine the quality of our LIVES.

    (Wow, are good ________ IMPORTANT!!)

23. When people borrow your stuff, they should __________ it promptly.

25. When a RUDE person wants you to be quiet, he or she will yell "Oh _ _ _ _ _ _ !" (Two words)

30. If you want people to know you are trustworthy, you must keep each ________. (It rhymes with *Thomas* and *bomb us.*)

DOWN

1. What do we call people who are NOT nice when they talk to us? (The correct answer is not "Jerks." The correct answer rhymes with *food.*)

2. An important person who is in your mirror.

3. Abbreviation for the United States.

4. What do we call people who vandalize other people's property? (It rhymes with *candles.*)

6. George Washington once said, "I cannot tell a ________, I chopped down the house!" (Or was it a cherry tree?)

8. Taking __________ is bad for your health. Selling them will get you into a juvenile detention center or prison.

9. You have a right to be treated fairly; you have a right not to be hurt; you have a right not to have your things stolen; you have a right not to be treated rudely. These are some of your ________.

10. Mom will think you are terrific if you offer to help ________ the dishes. (The answer is not "break." The answer rhymes with *moo.*)

14. If you are trustworthy, people will respect you and they will ________ you. (It rhymes with *must dust* the *crust.*)

15. If you take care of your health, you are less likely to get ________.

17. If you "put yourself in someone else's shoes" and try to understand their feelings, that means you have ________. (It is a VERY important word; it is VERY important to YOU.)

20. It makes us very sad when people ________ our feelings.

21. Having good values _____ good for YOU and good for your LIFE. (It rhymes with *fizz.*)

24. Opposite of "he."

26. "Oh, decisions, decisions. What to do, what _____ do!"

27. Opposite of "ma."

28. Not "down."

29. Abbreviation for New Orleans, and it's what you say to drugs.

# The American Dream:

## Should You Go For It?

Have you ever heard of "The American Dream"?

This is what is means:

Years ago, many people from Europe and other countries came to America for a better life.[1]

They wanted freedom.

They wanted to make a good life for themselves.

They wanted to be happy.

They were willing to work for it. They we willing to "Go for it!"

The good life that they wanted had a nickname. It was called "The American Dream."

[1] Although, as you know, many of our ancestors were forced to come to America to be slaves.

Nothing has changed. Absolutely nothing.

People still come to America to find The American Dream. *Americans want The American Dream, too.*

People still want to make a good life for themselves.

They still want freedom.

They still want to make their own choices.

They still want to be happy.

Which parts of the American Dream would you like for yourself and your future family?

Check which ones you would like.

Check them ALL, if you wish.

____ To have friends

____ To be loved

____ To be an informed, educated person

____ To have ability and skill

____ To have a good job or career

____ To be a trustworthy and responsible person

____ To have money and nice things

____ To earn respect and recognition

____ To have a good life

The American Dream is NOT just for rich people.

Or just for white people.

EVERYONE has an opportunity to make a good life for themselves.

Everyone has an opportunity to choose the kind of "good life" they would like.

But you have to "Go for it!"

You have to "Work for it!"

People want different things in life: "Different strokes for different folks."

- ✔ Some people mainly want a good job and a nice place to live for their family.
- ✔ Some people want an apartment in the city, with lots of shops and theaters.
- ✔ Some people want to live in the country. Maybe buy a horse.
- ✔ Some people don't care where they live—as long as they can go bowling or fishing or play tennis whenever they have time.
- ✔ Some people want to work extra hard and build their own business. They might have an appliance store, a video store, a restaurant, or a home decorating business.
- ✔✔ Most people want a job or career that they enjoy and that pays well.

**Check which is best.**

**______ An enjoyable life.**

**______ A difficult or miserable life.**

That wasn't a hard choice, was it?

## AN IMPORTANT LESSON (So listen up!!)

Have you heard people say this?

"YOU MAKE YOUR OWN LUCK!!"

What does this mean?

___

Have you heard people say this?

"THE HARDER I WORK, THE LUCKIER I GET!!"

What does this mean?

___

Both statements mean the SAME THING.

Both statements mean this:

If you want to succeed and have a good life, you can't just wait around, do nothing, and hope to "get lucky."

You are not going to win a million dollar lottery.

Stealing will land you in prison. Guaranteed.

You must decide what you want. Then "Go for it!" "Work for it!"

And the harder you work, the luckier you will get. Guaranteed

TRUST ME, IT'S WORTH IT! ☺☺

## WRITTEN TEST

The way to reach the American Dream is:

(Hint: Use the words "education," "work," and "Go for it!" And maybe "trustworthy" and "good values.")

____________________________________________________________

____________________________________________________________

____________________________________________________________

____________________________________________________________

Going for The American Dream includes two important points:

1. Right NOW, plan what will be best for YOU later. (Plan to graduate from high school. Plan to go to a technical school or college.)

2. Do NOT hurt—or destroy—your chances for a good life. (For example: Do NOT drop out of school. Do NOT become a criminal.)

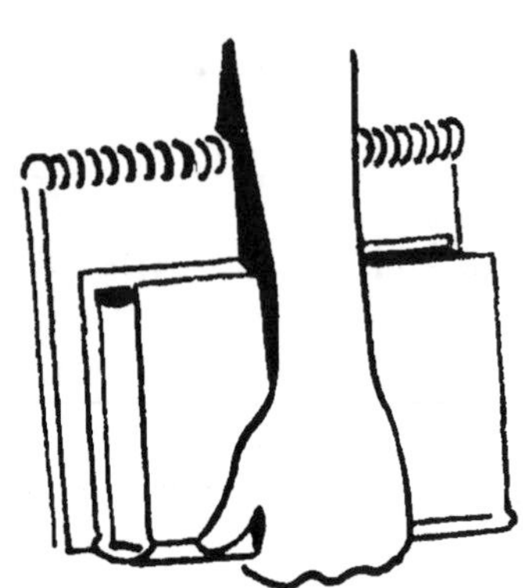

Remember Activity 1?

It was about CHOICES and DECISIONS.

Reaching the American Dream—living the life you WANT to live—means making GOOD CHOICES. Making GOOD DECISIONS.

It means WORKING for the life you want. Luck won't do it.

> **Remember:**
> **THE HARDER YOU WORK,**
> **THE LUCKIER YOU GET!**
> **And,**
> **YOU MAKE YOUR OWN LUCK!**

# Chapter 39

# WARNING! WARNING!

## People Are Playing with Your Head!

Let's be logical.
We learn our values from somewhere, right?

WHERE DO VALUES COME FROM?
We learn values from our PARENTS.
We learn values in SCHOOL and CHURCH.
We learn values from TV and MOVIES.
We learn values from our FRIENDS.
We are not BORN with good values or bad values.
They don't come from outer space.

Everybody likes television.
Everybody likes friends.

But TV and FRIENDS can do BIG TIME DAMAGE to your VALUES. And your values determine WHO you are. And WHAT you are. Values influence your DECISIONS and CHOICES.

**Values Affect Your LIFE!**

In the following, be logical.
Think about the best choices for YOU and YOUR LIFE.

***Important Idea*: Saturday cartoons are funny. And "action" TV shows are fun to watch. But they might teach you that VIOLENCE is a good idea. It isn't. (Even if Superheroes are violent.)**

Millions of kids watch Saturday morning cartoons. You probably watch them, too. Or maybe you did when you were younger.

Is there a lot of VIOLENCE on Saturday cartoons?
Are people punching and stabbing and shooting each other?

Yes _____ No _____

Are punching, stabbing, and shooting the BEST way to solve our everyday problems?

Yes _____ No _____

Some people learn that violence is a good way to solve problems.

They cause BIG-TIME problems for themselves and for others.
For example: In many big cities, people have shot each other dead over little traffic arguments. "Hey, you can't pull in front of me!" (✳✳Blam! Blam! Blam!✳✳) "So long, sucker!" (And for me it's off to prison for the rest of my life!!)

Good decision, right?

Wrong _____

Everybody watches "action" movies on TV and in theaters.
Like Batman and Indiana Jones. They are fun to watch. (I like them, too.)

Do you watch "action" movies on TV? Movies that show punching, shooting, stabbing, choking, and all that violent stuff?

Yes _____ No _____

Watching violence on TV can be fun.
But—PUH-LEESE—don't let "movie violence" teach you that violence is an OK way to think and to live.
Don't let "movie violence" teach you values that can hurt YOU or hurt OTHERS.

> ☛ VIOLENCE IS NOT A GOOD VALUE ☚
> **It is harmful to others. It is harmful to YOU.**

Imagine you have a disagreement with someone. Is the BEST solution to punch them in the face? Hit them with a chair? Stab them in the stomach? Shoot a hole in their head?

Yes _____ No _____

Some other solutions are:
Talk to them
Ignore them
Go away

Talk to a friend or relative
Do something else, something you enjoy

Violence is bad for everyone.

### *Important Idea:* TV Can Teach Other Bad Values.

MTV ("Music TV") is a show on cable TV.
It might be on too late for you to watch.
It mainly is a show for teenagers.

MTV is fun to watch.
It is entertaining.
It shows teenagers dancing to rock music and having fun.
Sometimes famous music groups perform.

MTV shows many teenage girls dressed in strange ways.
Like they are not wearing very much at all.

This helps entertain people who watch the show.
But MTV might teach girls that "not wearing very much" and "being sexy" are EXTREMELY important values. Not wearing much and being sexy are NOT important values for girls.

MTV might teach all teenagers that rock music and being a "great dancer" are more important than they really are.

What IS important is YOU.
What IS important is having values that help you live a good life.
Being a trustworthy and caring person.
Respecting yourself and earning the respect of others.
Getting an education and training.
And NOT being a loser.

Sooner or later you will watch MTV.
But keep MTV in its place.

It's fun to watch.
But don't let MTV teach you that girls must be sexy.
That rock music and being a good dancer are the most important things in the world.

YOU and WHAT KIND OF PERSON YOU BECOME are the most important things in YOUR life.

***Important Idea*: Friends Can Teach Us GOOD Values.**
**Friends Can Teach Us HARMFUL, HURTFUL Values.**

When you become a teenager, you will do what your friends do.
This is called "conformity."
Do you know the word *conformity*?
*Conformity* means being like other people.
Conformity means DOING what others DO.
Sometimes we even THINK like others THINK.
We "conform" so that others will accept us and like us.

Conformity is perfectly normal.
We all conform to what others expect of us.

Have you noticed that teenagers seem to dress alike?
Listen to the same music?
Talk the same way?
Do the same things?
If somebody paints their hair green—bingo, 200 green heads!
(If they are members of a gang, they will all dress in the same way. They will all use the same drugs. They will all hate members of other gangs.)

Conformity is normal.
We ALL want to be liked by our friends.

And so we DO what our friends want us to DO.
We THINK what our friends want us to THINK.

This is fine—if our friends have values like:

Honesty
Trustworthiness
Helping others
Pleasantness
Good manners
Good health
Keeping the environment clean
Getting an education and professional training

As they say in Jamaica, "No problem, Mon!"

But what if our teenage friends value shoplifting, lying and cheating, rudeness, leaving messes, taking drugs, getting drunk, carrying guns, and dropping out of school?

And some teenagers don't THINK about the CONSEQUENCES of their ACTIONS.

Think about it. Can we have a terrific future family life if we commit CRIMES that will land us in PRISON?

Yes _____ No _____

Can we have a terrific future life if we have no TRAINING and cannot find a job that will pay enough MONEY to live on?

Yes _____ No _____

Can we have a terrific future life if we ruin our HEALTH?

Yes _____ No _____

Let's get back to CONFORMITY.
What will YOU do if your friends have values that are hurtful and self-destructive?

Will you do what is best for yourself and your life?

Yes _____ No _____

Or will you do what your (loser) friends want you to do?

Yes _____ No _____

Chapter

# 40

# Final Examination:

## Values and Your Dreams

---

Let's think about decisions and choices that can help you reach YOUR dreams. (You can call it The American Dream, if you want to.)

Let's think about things that will HELP or HURT your chances for a good future life.

> **You just have to use common sense.**
> **Just think a little bit. It won't hurt.**

Think about "good values" and "bad values."
Ask yourself these questions:

Does this hurt other people?

Does it hurt me?

Can it hurt my life?

Would my mother, grandmother, or teacher do this?

If I do this, would my family, my friends, and other people lose respect for me?

As you read each statement, ask yourself:

Will this activity probably HELP my chances for a good future life?
(Will this ACTION have GOOD CONSEQUENCES for me?)

Or will it HURT my chance for a GOOD future life—for the YEARS and YEARS and YEARS that I will be an adult.
(Will this ACTION have BAD CONSEQUENCES for me?)

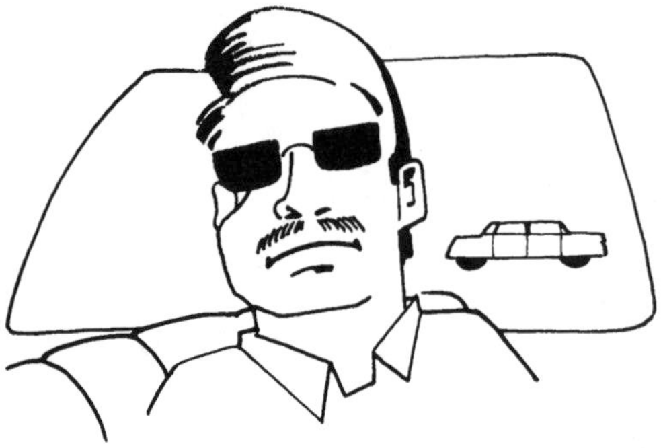

| | Will HELP My Life | Will HURT My Life |
|---|---|---|
| 1. Jake drives a big Cadillac. He got the money by selling drugs. I would like to be like Jake. | ________ | ________ |
| 2. It would be just fine to get caught selling drugs and go to prison for a few years. | ________ | ________ |
| 3. I will try to develop ALL the skills and abilities I can—in reading, writing, math, science, computers, and music. And in swimming, basketball, and other sports, too. | ________ | ________ |

| | Will HELP My Life | Will HURT My Life |
|---|---|---|
| 4. I don't care about my health. The important thing is to have fun. | ________ | ________ |
| 5. The TV cartoon boy Bart Simpson doesn't work hard in school. He is "Proud to be an Underachiever." I should be like Bart Simpson. | ________ | ________ |
| 6. There is nothing wrong with a little stealing and burglary when I get bigger. I won't get caught. Besides, they don't do anything to kids. | ________ | ________ |
| 7. I plan to work hard in school, then go on to technical school or college, then get a good job. | ________ | ________ |
| 8. When I get a little older, I plan to carry a gun to school—then I'll be grown up and powerful! I'll get respect! | ________ | ________ |
| 9. I want others to know that I am a good person, someone who is honest and trustworthy. | ________ | ________ |
| 10. Smoking is really cool, even if it does cause cancer and heart problems. | ________ | ________ |
| 11. It's a good idea to be a nasty, grouchy, sarcastic person—and maybe a bully too. | ________ | ________ |

| | Will HELP My Life | Will HURT My Life |
|---|---|---|
| 12. It's a good idea to be honest and fair with other people. It's just the right way to live. People will respect me more, too. | ________ | ________ |
| 13. It's good to have empathy, to try to understand other people's feelings. | ________ | ________ |
| 14. It's okay to steal and destroy other people's property. In fact, it's fun. | ________ | ________ |
| 15. It's best to respect other people's rights, to return their things, and not to damage their property. (Because that's how I want to be treated!) | ________ | ________ |
| 16. It's good to think about my future life—and NOT make BIG mistakes that will trash it (like dropping out of school, or becoming a drug dealer or a criminal). | ________ | ________ |

| | Will HELP My Life | Will HURT My Life |
|---|---|---|
| 17. Friends and people who love you are valuable. You should treat them with honesty, fairness, and friendliness. | ________ | ________ |
| 18. For girls, the most important thing in life is to try to be really, really sexy. | ________ | ________ |
| 19. If my friends want me to have bad values—like being rude, taking drugs, and dropping out of school—I should do whatever my friends want me to. | ________ | ________ |
| 20. If I develop abilities and skills, I can get a good-paying job. I can buy nice things. | ________ | ________ |
| 21. It doesn't matter if I lie, cheat, steal, don't return things, and don't show up on time. Who cares if I am irresponsible? | ________ | ________ |
| 22. I don't need to think about other people's rights to fair and pleasant treatment. That's their problem! | ________ | ________ |

Answers: I hope you know all of the right answers. Your values and your future life depend on it.

We will end our book with two terrific lines from the movie, *Back to the Future, Part III.*
First, Doc says, "We all make decisions that affect the course of our lives."
Later, he says, "Your future is whatever you make it—so make it a good one!"
Doc is a very smart man!

**☺Good luck with your life!☺**

# Solutions to Puzzles

Chapter 4. Word Search About Values

|  | F |  |  |  |  |  |  |  |  |  |
|---|---|---|---|---|---|---|---|---|---|---|
| T | R | U | S | T | W | O | R | T | H | Y |
|  | I |  |  | H |  | V | I |  | E | E |
| H | E | D | O | O | G | A | G |  | L | D |
| O | N |  |  | U |  | L | H |  | P | U |
| N | D |  |  | G |  | U | T |  | F | C |
| E | L |  |  | H |  | E |  |  | U | A |
| S | Y |  |  | T |  | S |  |  | L | T |
| T |  |  |  | F | A | I | R |  |  | I |
|  |  |  |  | U | W | R | O | N | G | O |
|  | H | E | A | L | T | H |  |  |  | N |

← DOOG = GOOD

Chapter 19. Crossword Puzzle: Rights and Values

| | | | 1 L | 2 I | 3 B | | | | | 4 H | U | 5 M |
|---|---|---|---|---|---|---|---|---|---|---|---|---|
| 6 D | E | C | I | S | I | O | N | 7 S | | I | | E |
| | | | T | | G | | | N | | | | S |
| 8 H | U | 9 R | T | | | 10 C | H | O | I | 11 C | E | S |
| U | | 12 I | L | L | | H | | O | | A | | |
| 13 R | U | D | E | | | 14 E | M | P | 15 A | T | 16 H | Y |
| T | | | | 17 Y | | A | | | L | | E | |
| | 18 H | O | N | E | S | T | | 19 F | A | I | R | |
| | E | | | S | | E | | I | | | | 20 H |
| 21 G | A | N | 22 G | | 23 D | R | U | G | 24 S | | 25 M | E |
| | L | | R | | A | | G | | T | | 26 A | L |
| | 27 T | W | O | | 28 V | A | L | U | E | S | | P |
| 29 A | H | | U | | E | | Y | | A | | | U |
| C | | | C | | | 30 A | | | 31 L | 32 I | 33 E | S |
| T | | | 34 H | U | R | T | | | | 35 S | D | |

Chapter 31. Word Search for Friendly, Caring Words

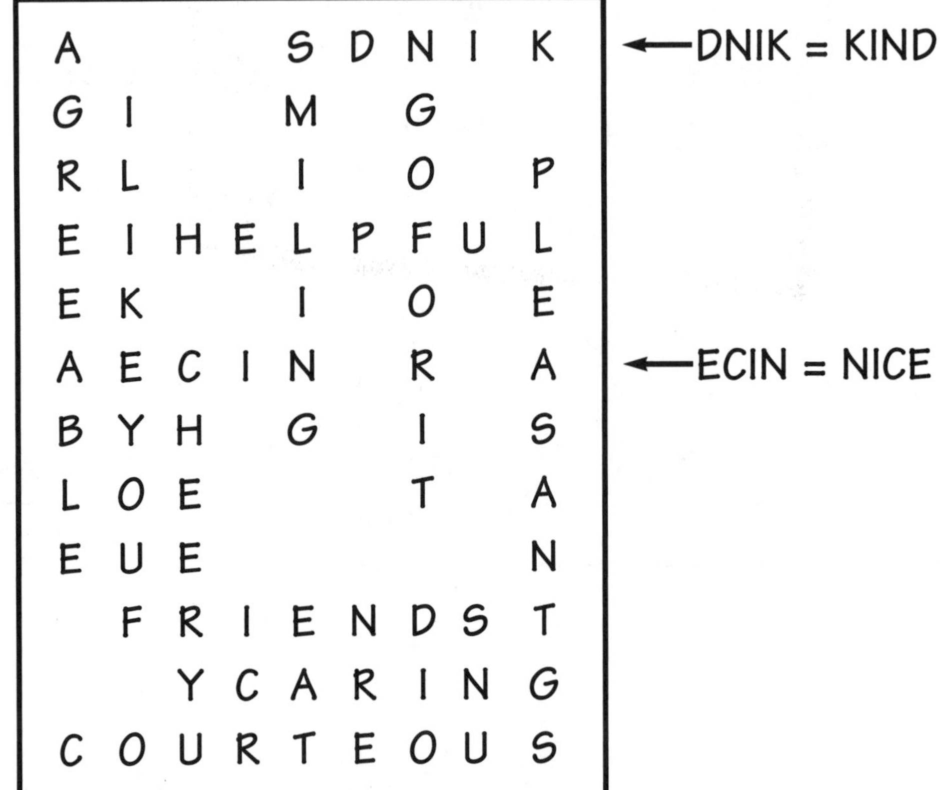

Chapter 32. Word Search for Rude, Hurtful Words

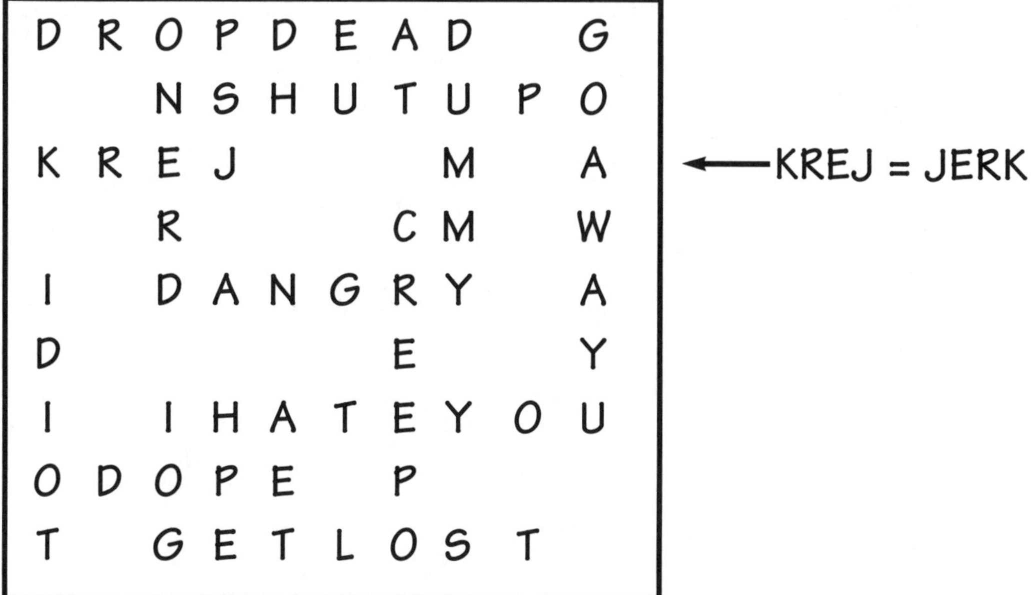


Chapter 37. Crossword Puzzle: Your Basic Good Values

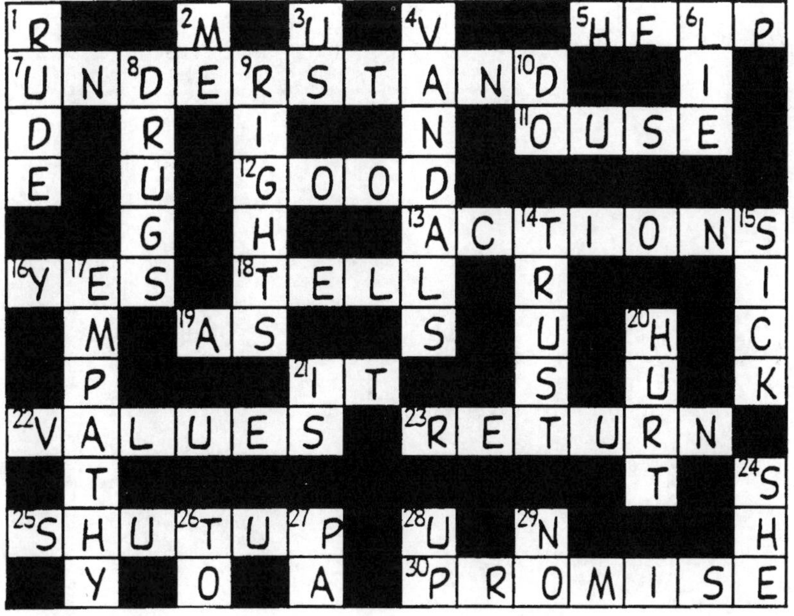